COSMICALLY CURIOUS

To: James Powell
Oct. 5, 2021

Leonard M. Jordan

COSMICALLY CURIOUS

Perceptions from a Speck Called Earth

Len Jepson

TRUE DIRECTIONS
AN AFFILIATE OF TARCHER PERIGEE | iUniverse®

COSMICALLY CURIOUS
PERCEPTIONS FROM A SPECK CALLED EARTH

iUniverse books may be ordered through booksellers or by contacting:

iUniverse
1663 Liberty Drive
Bloomington, IN 47403
www.iuniverse.com
1-800-Authors (1-800-288-4677)

ISBN: 978-1-5320-4487-8 (sc)
ISBN: 978-1-5320-4486-1 (hc)
ISBN: 978-1-5320-4485-4 (e)

Library of Congress Control Number: 2018902880

Print information available on the last page.

iUniverse rev. date: 04/23/2018

To Linda and our daughter and son-in-law, Abigail and Mat Berry, who have grown from groans over my puns to creating their own homespun ones.

Contents

Preface

Early on, when I was about four years old, there were people who thought I must be adopted. My dad, mom, and sister seemed normal. In contrast, I and our adopted dogs were a little weird. Our dogs and I were as curious as our adopted cats.

One evening when I was about 4.4 years old, our Lutheran bishop came to dinner at our house. I asked my dad if I could say the table prayer. He said, "Sure."

My prayer went like this: "Holy Spirit, nice and brown. Amen."

The bishop said, "What did he say?"

My dad said, "We sometimes don't know."

I likely was carrying some of my Sunday school learnings into a realm of philosophy called ontology, a study of the nature of being with ideas concerning what mysteries surround us or may be said to exist.

For example: "Philip said to him, 'Lord, show us the

Father, and we will be satisfied.' Jesus said to him, 'Have I been with you all this time, Philip, and you still do not know me? Whoever has seen me has seen the Father. How can you say, "Show us the Father"?'" (John 14:8–9). Ontology asks questions such as "Is Jesus saying that he has the same substance or essence of the Father?"

As one goes one more step, ontology is especially significant in relation to the Holy Trinity as Christians attempt to articulate how the Father, the Son, and the Holy Spirit are all the same substance or essence.

There was on our table that evening a fresh, just-out-of-the-oven loaf of brown bread with a wonderful aroma. In Sunday school we were taught that the Holy Spirit is a wind or a breath or a fragrant breeze that brings life and that Jesus is the bread of life. Holy Spirit, nice and brown.

Philosophical thoughts at age 4.4? You betcha. Children are curious. It's called epistemic curiosity.

It is typical for curiosity to increase early in life and decrease as life goes on. A study found that, on average, curiosity increases from age twelve until people attend college (McCrae, 2002).

Another study documents that some people retain their curiosity as they grow older. Common characteristics of these people include rich emotional lives with both positive and negative feelings. These people have an active search for meaning in life, are not restricted by social norms, and pursue careers that provide opportunities to be independent and creative (Kashdan and Silvia, 2009). What a relief it has been to know that I am weirdly curious, decade after decade, in a good and positive way. I have always been epistemically curious, and I carry out this orientation in ways that I did as a young child. I continue to act like a kid. I love to laugh with others at conventions, with homilies, and on other playgrounds of life.

Individuals are born creative from the get-go, with unleashed minds. I believe it is unfortunate that as some people advance in years, many of them are collared with a restrictive leash, which limits the childlike enthusiasm to play, to be called into the proverbial principal's office, to have fun exploring, or even to question the world around us. Albert Einstein believed that imagination is more important than knowledge. This is because knowledge is limited. Imagination embraces the entire cosmos and is the essential element in creativity.

I personally believe that life can be enriched with an epistemic epidemic that can include humor. After all, comedy fits so well with curiosity; humor by definition is a keen perception of the ludicrous or incongruous.

I do establish limits for my childlike humorous behavior. I know that some professors, bishops, parishioners, or people at large are somewhat solemn and can identify with only small doses of creative humor. It is rewarding when I counterbalance stoics correctly with intentional minimized humor and then see them softly react with a faint smirk when nobody is looking.

Linda and I promoted this epistemic curiosity with young confirmation students as we team-taught for twenty-five years, beginning in the early 1970s. We realized that educational systems often lacked the ideal of encouraging young people to bring their own questions. Curricula had scripted questions with predetermined answers, which could ultimately be parroted in front of church leaders and parents on fright night, the evening before the day of confirmation. We taught not by spoon-feeding mesmerizing memorization but instead by providing four or five learning styles so diverse students could be highly engaged for at least a fourth or a fifth of the time instead of being put to sleep.

Even before ordination on June 21, 1970, I began to prepare for a wide professional role in a variety of disciplines. These came to be realized in parish, synodical, regional, state, national, and ultimately global involvements in Finland, Hong Kong, Germany, South Africa, and Japan—including leisure/recreation development, mission development, community development, ecumenical and interreligious dialogues, stewardship studies, communication theory (journalism and radio/television production), and the global emerging church movement.

My personhood as a Lutheran pastor has, at times, incorrectly labeled me to be very boring and parochial. Instead, my style grows out of playful passions for liberal expansions in theology, philosophy, sociology, ecumenical and interreligious leadership, and tastes of physics. These fields of study have most recently led to my explorations into cosmological theories and quantum and holographic theologies.

To embrace curiosity is to break from past certainties. All of us tend to love certainty because it gives us confidence.

But certainty can become a haven for worn-out or mistaken ideas. Dogmatism, the tendency to lay down principles as absolutely true without consideration of evidence or the opinions of others, divides. In contrast, curiosity builds bridges that link to exciting new places.

World-historical changes occur as centuries go by. We are impacted by these societal changes in dramatic ways today, convincingly portrayed by the mind-set of millennials, individuals born during the years from 1977 through 1992.

Today's changing cultures bring uncertainties, causing older generations to turn inward and become more insular. In contrast, millennials maintain a more open, broad, and diverse stance, which can benefit all of us.

Cosmically Curious: Perceptions from a Speck Called Earth serves as an introduction to these dynamic changes of the past and present and is a catalyst that encourages openness to them as they continue to unfold.

Acknowledgments

I am very grateful for many mentors who have provided unique settings for my professional development, especially Pastor Jack Nitz, internship supervisor; Giles Ekola and Pastor Bill Bruggeman, Douglas County, Minnesota, team ministry; Deacon Joseph Trimboli; Pastor F. Dean Lueking, sabbatical coordinator; Pastor Olli Valtonen, Helsinki and Pastor John LeMond, Hong Kong.

Special appreciation also goes to parishioners of First English Evangelical Lutheran Church of Mishawaka, Indiana, for their contributions in this book: Richard Allen, Eric Petersen, Kathryn Coleman, Jean Whetstone, Mark and Aurora Nieding, and Ann Umbaugh.

The technological skills of Rich Hall were outstanding for producing this book, especially as he calmly confronted the loss of the first draft, which sizzled as I accidently spilled a full pilsner glass of beer on that computer, which now rests in a junkyard.

Introduction

The important thing is not to stop questioning.
Curiosity has its own reason for existence. One
cannot help but be in awe when he contemplates
the mysteries of eternity, of life, of the marvelous
structure of reality. It is enough if one tries merely
to comprehend a little of this mystery each day.

—Einstein, 1955

Cosmically Curious can be a convincer for being very
curious about everything. It can change one's views
of existence, which can be fun, strange, or creepy.
Philosophies, theologies, and physics combine to reveal
new curiosities about consciousness.

Human beings tend to assume what is called daily life
and activities to be well defined and without question.
Curiosity, on the other hand, can be compared to the way
an artist looks at the world, preparing to put it on canvas.
Streets, sidewalks, trees, buildings, cans of cream-style

corn, school buses, mosquitoes, God, people, and even one's own identity are not taken for granted. Instead, imagination calls for certain types of brushes that bring new strokes, the metaphorical and mysterious mix of colors, the differing lights, and casts of shadows.

If there is anything we feel with certainty, it is that the world we experience is real. Each morning we take for granted that the iPhone with the alarm set for 6:00 a.m. is real. We can see, touch, and hear it and turn it off. We can climb into a vehicle and drive to work. We can observe the yellow arches of McDonald's still lighted in the predawn grayness and a myriad of lighted arch rivals. It seems without question that out there, around us, independent and apart from us, exists a physical world, totally real, solid, and tangible.

It is curious that this is not so. It's accurate to say that there seems to be a physical world.

It seems that we are directly experiencing the world. It seems that the colors we see and the sounds we hear are there, around us, just as we experience them. But even an elementary philosophical study of the processes of perception show us that we likely are mistaken.

We can choose to meander along familiar paths that may not end but may have never existed. Or we can open ourselves to cosmic truths that can change the ways we observe. As a result, we begin to manifest a new experience and become open to a broader view of reality.

When we embrace these expanded views, the cosmos becomes less defined by divisive prejudices, which can become the last gasp of human enlightenment.

Each chapter's subject(s) in this book is prefaced in italic print, which can be a foundation for further studies or discussion starters for group conversations.

Scripture quotations are from Revised Standard Version, Thomas Nelson & Sons (Toronto, New York, Edinburgh, 1953).

1

Perceptions of Reality and Heuristics

At any given moment, a perception of reality is given shape by complex constructs. These constructs can include some or many of the following from this short list of possible ingredients:

- *Ideologies: Bodies of doctrines, myths, beliefs, and so forth, that guide individuals, social movements, institutions, social classes, or groups. Ideologies are generally taken to be prescriptive.*

- *Metaphysics (a subfield of philosophy): A study of the most general features of reality, such as existence, time, the relationship between mind and body, objects, and their properties, wholes and their parts, events, processes, and causations.*

- *Physical cosmology: The study of the origin, evolution, dynamics, and ultimate fate of the universe and the scientific laws governing these considerations.*

- *Religious/mythological cosmologies: Bodies of beliefs based on the historical, mythological, religious, and esoteric (i.e., with meaning for only a few) literature and traditions of creation and eschatology, theologies concerned with death, judgment, and the final destiny of the cosmos, such as:*

  ○ *Hindu cosmology, dated 2000 BC, is cyclical or oscillating, with one cycle of existence being about 311 trillion years and the life of one universe around 8 billion years, including an infinite number of universes at one given time.*

  ○ *Biblical cosmology, dated with the Genesis creation narrative (c. 500 BC) is based on Babylonian cosmology (c. 3000 BC), with the flat earth floating in infinite waters of chaos.*

  ○ *Multiversal cosmology. Fakr al-Din al-Razi, a Persian Sunni Muslim theologian and philosopher (1149–1209), submitted the idea that there is an infinite outer space beyond the known world and that God has the power to fill this vacuum with an infinite number of universes.*

o   *Big bang theory (Friedmann-Lemaitre Model),*
    1927–29. Lemaitre is considered to be the father
    of the big bang model.

o   *Eternal inflation, Andrei Linde, 1983. This is*
    a multiverse system, with some expanding into
    bubble universes supposedly like our entire
    cosmos.

I'm fortunate to have many unique settings and mentors who brought and bring new shapes to my thinking. At the same time, I make sure that I do not miss the traditional education, resources, and images. I take verbatim notes, sit in the front seats of lecture halls and tour buses, write summaries of each textbook's pages on the margins, and sometimes take on the look of an orthodox, knowledge-filled Lutheran pastor with colorful stoles and chasubles. I even listened intently in grade school to Miss Rowe's teaching out there in the classroom from the confines of the coatroom, standing in there for punishment with cocomedian Scott Harding and a few other classmates following our predictable but class-interruptive behaviors.

But instead of simply hanging out in isolated but admirable places like coatrooms, I love heuristics, a trial-and-error path that leads toward a goal that is not clear.

To live life without a specific direction is quite joyful, for it is full of surprises.

These new adventures are detour routes that are messy and muddy, untidy, cluttered, sloppy, dusty, and bumpy. They are the metaphorical highways of curiosity! To travel heuristically is to love orange detour signs. As a kid, I was always filled with great joy when orange detour signs would be set up on our family's chosen highways from Minnesota to visit my Detroit uncle and aunt and cousins. Back then the signs were enigmatically lighted by round oil lamps. At dusk, the flames and their smoke introduced a haunting obscurity about the road ahead.

The mysterious adventures of traveling those detours through forgotten little villages with people sitting on their front porches waving at multitudes of newcomers in buses and trucks and automobiles opened whole new worlds to the travelers as well as otherwise-isolated villagers.

I still love detour signs. They invite us to learn in a nondogmatic fashion. Detours encourage learners to explore without the confines of an interstate highway or a global positioning system or back seat drivers. Of course, GPS voices are very mild-mannered, pleasant, patient, and understanding, but I really prefer the two-way conversational one-on-one voices of detour flag women.

The heuristic method is not anti-presuppositional or antitraditional but opens a route of discovery where people are given the tools to learn for themselves even when the detour ends and there is a return to the familiar road. The heuristic method is one of ideas with new and broader horizons.

Ecumenical, interreligious, and pluralistic conversations or thoughts that often occur on the detours can lead to new concepts created by looking at things in novel ways. The heuristic style is also called lateral thinking and sideways thinking.

This valuable variable provokes fresh ideas or changes the frames of reference. Otherwise, more normal logical, vertical thinking simply carries a chosen idea forward.

On a personal level, my sideways thinking is replicated by our daughter, Abby. We enjoy laughing about the ways we think.

One day my wife Linda called my iPhone. I was driving, so at the red light I answered. Sure enough, the conversation spurred me on to sideways thinking and spiced up our consciousnesses.

Linda said, "On your way home, pick up a jar of whole coriander and some fresh thyme." I immediately imagined that this would uniquely cause me to arrive home later than

I had planned. Why? Because I would have to meander to find the coriander and it would take even more time to find the thyme.

Vertical thinking tends to be repetitious and boring and robotic. Vertical thinking responses can go like this: Okay. I'll get the coriander and some thyme because the light is green.

2

Where Is Reality? The Philosophies of Sense Perception

Consciousness is given shape by complexities that go beyond ideologies, metaphysics, and cosmologies. There are questions about how mental processes and symbols depend on the world internal and external to the perceiver.

The majority of people on earth wake up each morning and assume existence to be ad infinitum work, play, surroundings, communities, education, nurturing, or mowing one's lawn. One then simply labels all thoughts and all perceptions "life"—and generally life means what one sees, hears, smells, tastes, and touches.

On the other hand, the word philosophy *calls attention to speculation. The word comes from* philo *and* sophia, *love and wisdom. Philosophy is the love of wisdom, which includes pursuit, inquiry, and study.*

When we become cosmically curious and have questions

about reality, the field of metaphysics suspiciously wonders about the most basic features of reality, such as existence itself, time, and the relationship between mind and body.

Let's get on the bus! Buckle up! I love buses! I used to drive a ninety-passenger school bus down assumed streets in St. Paul, Minnesota. But now I invite you to board one that travels along metaphorical highways!

Philosophies of sense perception focus on the nature of conscious experience and are contextualized in two different ways. Idealism is the theory that reality is mentally construed, an internal perceptual copy generated by neural processes in the brain. Realism holds that reality, or at least some part of it, exists independently of the brain.

Direct (naïve) realism counters indirect (representational) realism. Indirect realism is the position that our conscious experience is not of the real world external but an internal representation, a tiny virtual reality replica. Both direct and indirect realism acknowledge that there is a world external.

The most common philosophical theory of sense perception is direct (naïve) realism. When people don't recall the science of biology, they take this childish theory into adult life. This theory regards sense perception to be directly of the external world.

Scottish philosopher Thomas Reid (1710–1796)

advanced this theory, saying that sensation is composed of a set of data transfers that, in some way, are transparent, allowing a direct connection between perception and the world, a direct naïve realism.

Indirect (representational) realism is much more at home with my thinking. This holds that we can only be aware of external objects by realizing representations. Over the years I have become comfortable with directly saying that indirect realism is really the way to go.

Again, indirect realism holds that sense perceptions only represent external realities. In somewhat of an amusing way, these representations of the external bring wonderment. Sometimes the representations are freaky and weird; other representations are sophisticated and beautiful. Over the long run, however, we cannot claim that representations of the external are one or the other.

I recall an example of indirect realism from the late 1950s in Altona, Illinois.

Many of us students rode in a school bus, at least a representation of a school bus, which continues to push my funny bone to this day. This thing, represented as a 1951 International with a Wayne Body was mysteriously … there.

This thing was a forty-two-passenger faded yellow

perception. Its suspension springs in the back were too hefty, causing the rear to be maintained about four feet higher than its front. The left front spring was obviously either broken or very weak, causing the whole thing to list to the left.

Its wheels were unusually small, causing the perception of wheel wells to have no relationship to the wheels and having no reason to be. The long exhaust pipe was located at a normal height from the ground, thanks to the longest strap hanger I have ever perceived.

The driver, Carl McClay, was also a Lutheran farmer. I enjoyed Sunday afternoon family drives even more when we would drive by his farm, for he parked this thing near his barn. Just to observe this thing sitting motionless was pleasurable.

Carl was not tall or short. His driver's seat behind an enormous steering wheel was only 2.7 inches off the floor. With difficulty he could peer through the spokes of the steering wheel and have a view of the road ahead through the very lowest portion of the windshield.

It was especially frustrating for him in a heavy rain downpour or snowstorm, for the windshield wipers, suspended on arms attached at the top of the vehicle, were unusually short, leaving the lower portion of the windshield untouched.

To sit in the back seats was comparable to being in the back seats of a movie theater with twenty-first-century stadium seating, and even higher on the extremely elevated right side. It was somewhat frightening to barrel down narrow US Highway 34 at fifty-five miles per hour, especially not being able to see Carl down there in front very near the floor.

This is, by the way, as are all of my stories, cosmically true.

It was also my delight at a younger age to live down the street in Montevideo, Minnesota, from a charter bus driver. He always parked it in front of his house on North Sixth Street. Again, his thing in any realm of direct realism would be questionable.

This item had silver, scroll-like designs on the sides, was too tall for its width, and had the entrance/exit door well behind the front wheel well. But most amazing was the location of the gear shift. It was perceived to be about 4.3 feet long, with a crook in the middle, immediately behind the driver's seat.

I enjoyed watching this act, with the driver trying to look at the street ahead, slightly turned in his seat, attempting to reach the gear shift behind him as he manipulated his feet on the clutch and accelerator.

Montevideo, sister city of Montevideo, Uruguay, is impressive but quite small compared to her South American sister. This explains why she had only one city bus. I will never forget that it was constantly, and I mean constantly, being repaired. In fact, the vertical hood, with license plate, taillights, brake lights, and turn-signal lights that covered the rear-mounted engine, was never shut, saving some time for the mechanics. Of course, the license plate and lights on the opened, horizontally positioned hood could only be seen from the air.

Going back to direct realism and indirect realism, these two are called realist philosophical theories of sense perception because they postulate that there is a world external to the mind. Direct realism says that one's perception of an object is exactly the way the object is out there. Indirect realism contends that the perception of an object out there is brain activity.

These three bus stories indeed favor for me an indirect realism track. Direct realism would support the manufacture or the sale of these things only by saying that, for some odd reason, these three buses out there are monstrosities and that they were sold at night on an unlighted bus lot. On the other hand, indirect realism could optimistically explain that they were sold by a bus salesperson who suggested that, in reality, these buses were possibly much better than they looked.

3

The World of Solipsism

It can be comforting to hear that both direct and indirect realism postulate that there is a world external to the mind, that we're sometimes passengers in some kind of thing. But don't sit back in your seat and leave the driving to Carl. Welcome to the world of solipsism.

This is the speculation that nothing can be proven to exist outside one's own mind. The word solipsism *comes from the Latin phrase* solus ipse, *which means "myself alone."*

Solipsism denies that houses, cities, buses, newspapers, kids, malls, colleges, pubs, and spouses have a real, independent existence. Instead, they are conceptions in one's mind, much like objects on a movie screen that appear to be real but are just projected. Solipsism says that a mind *is* the projector in one's theater in which no one else is present and there is a need for only one box of popcorn.

Solipsism holds that the entire cosmos and everything in it is created by the subconscious of the individual.

Solipsism can be traced back to Rene Descartes's famous statement, "I think, therefore I am!" This celebrates that one can be sure of her/his own existence because she/he is thinking and able to be doubting, because thoughts and doubts must have a source. So, can one then be sure that anything else exists? No.

Absolute solipsism is the stance that the mind is the only thing that exists. Trees, the sky, the earth, people, exhaust pipes and mufflers, interstate highways, ants, uncles, ladybugs, gentlemen bugs, and one's own body are perceived by one's subconscious mind.

Philosophical solipsism can become more understood by "us" as we consider the infant's solipsist view of life. An infant human being crawls through unknowns, alone, looking for meaning and connectivity. As an infant matures, solipsism is replaced with the belief that others share an intrinsic experience.

Glimmers of the solipsist perspective do continue to play in adulthood in the religiosity of the status quo. This can be represented with the conviction that only "my God" exists or that gays are an abomination. The addiction to iPhones and texting can also transport one to a solipsist philosophy, denying that signal lights and speed limits and cross-traffic independently exist.

There, of course (duh!), are not many true solipsists. It is curious that the most popular and legitimate solipsist for consideration could be the deity of Judaism, Christianity, and Islam. These cousin faith traditions claim that the deity creates (his) own world and all the acts in it; therefore, the solipsism philosophy could say that the world, the adherents of the traditions, and all the acts are in the mind of the deity.

4

Taking a Walk Down the Sidewalks and Edge-Thinking

Consideration of these far-out complexities of sense perception are connected to visits all of us seem to make with our optometrists, audiologists, and other health care practitioners who check out our senses.

When we seem to walk down the sidewalks, we do experience the external world mostly through our five senses: sight, sound, smell, touch, and taste. The reality is, however, that human beings, dogs, cats, squirrels, gnats, and mosquitos do not perceive the external world in parallel ways. Creatures who have the sense of sight serve as an example.

What one is looking at forms on the back of an eye, and this image is then turned into an electrical signal that is sent to a brain. The brain of a Swede and the brain of a

Norwegian elkhound then construct the data in very diverse ways.

In either case, there is no evidence of a real, corporate world. Carried another step, it can be entertained that it goes against common sense to suppose there is a material world, for we have no direct experience of it with any of the senses.

The perception of reality problem continues to this day. The identification of the problem generally goes to Rene Descartes when he asked how the material mind can connect to the assumed material external reality. He ultimately identified the tiny pineal gland as the point of contact between the two.

The pineal gland is one of several endocrine glands, glands that produce secretions that are distributed by way of the bloodstream. Because it is perceived to be the size of a pea, not much was known about this gland until the 1960s. It had become the object of mythical theories. Descartes called it "the seat of the soul."

In modern times philosophers and scientists propose other interactionist models. Their attempts to explain the mysterious problems of consciousness and psycho-physical relations between mind and the external lead them to explain the mystery with mysteries.

Every supposed perception of the world around us likely is not of the world out there. Perhaps there is not a world out there. Or perhaps you're not out there. To be fair, perhaps I'm not at all.

I concerned myself with these philosophical curiosities at a very young age and became a philosophy major and felt finally at home with reading the great philosophers as they delved into major curiosities about reality.

Many of us philosophy majors tend to live with normal and assumed experiences and then a myriad of far-out speculations about reality. This even includes reconstructed ways of observing what may be out there. I came to secretly describe myself as an *edge-thinker*.

I have never abandoned this second component of thinking. I have, however, discovered many years later that this is indeed related to a documented philosophical practice called TAE, Thinking at the Edge, developed by Eugene Gendlin and based on his philosophy of the implicit.

TAE is a path into unexpressed fields and unexpected depth. It brings one to walk on the edge of an implicit knowing and an explicit form. This method builds theories about reality.

I believe this edge-thinking focuses on the unclear

and yet demanding sense that there is much more than explicit thinking or knowledge that a person can make known with verbal statements. Gendlin says that the implicit has no words ... yet. TAE says that when we give full voice to the uniqueness of our own experience, we will become more resilient in standing up against even subtle authoritarianism. For example, speaking from my clergy profession, it is normal to simply give lip service to concepts from the recognized authority sources. One of the reasons for this is that implicit thinking does not easily fit into the existing logic or common discourse (Gendlin, 2004).

I tend to have some difficulty as an edge-thinker in believing that the external earth is possibly not flat. Perhaps the possibility that we are on a ball that seems to roar through an endless cosmos is too frightening.

This fear is minimized with our living in Mishawaka. It just seems safer to live in Mishawaka on good, flat solid dirt or riding on the commuter rail to Chicago's Loop on tracks built on solid flat terrains for the trains.

After all, Mishawaka's landscape is perceived to be so flat that it seems unfair that we should be required to pay for parking brakes on our vehicles, although they are useful during road trips. A problem living as a flat lander, however, is with flying. When Linda and I flew eastward to Hong Kong and then flew eastward out of Hong Kong to arrive in South Bend/Mishawaka, we arrived from the west.

This flat landscape even changes the way we speak in northern Indiana. We tend to invite people to visit not by saying "come on down" or "come on up" but instead by saying "come over."

This flip-flop, normal/far-out lifestyle for me in the 1960s presented my presence on the college campus during the daytime as a fairly normal, Swedish Lutheran student, questionable only to the extent that Concordia College was founded by Norwegian Lutherans.

This suspicion stems from the fact that Swedes and Norwegians in Minnesota don't get along that well. This was the reason why, with my dad being a pastor of a Swedish Lutheran Church, that as a kid I considered it appropriate to walk on the other side of the street in front of the Norwegian Lutheran church 1.6 blocks from our Swedish Lutheran parsonage.

Anyway, the other side of living on the edge happened when our philosophy classes were held during the nighttime in a cosmically friendly coffee house with dim lights and heavy, drawn, and musty drapes. I would sometimes imagine that if a blind philosophy major from Venice would be part of the gathering in this dark space she would be a perfect fit. We were a diverse lot and celebrated being "a little different" and would welcome the Venetian blind.

Our professor would introduce really far-out concepts, ask for responses, and then exhale and fill the confined space of overstuffed couches with his thick cigar smoke as he would toothily smile, nod his head up and down several times, and then wait for our speculations. It was another world!

This on-the-edge orientation provides a most difficult standard for discussing philosophical ideas with people of other interests. But they are so neat and cool! The important thing to remember is to realize that philosophical speculation requires one to dismiss normal life experiences. Edge-thinking is contagious.

Indeed, it came to be a fulfilling feeling for me as I seemed to walk around campus, sensing some people pauses with side glances that seemed to say, "He has to be a philosophy major." Perhaps this recognition stemmed from my wearing a French beret as I carried six or even eleven philosophy books in my bulging briefcase. Or perhaps this attention was even drawn with my being the only student to drive a car on campus, likely because there are only sidewalks on the Concordia College campus in Moorhead, Minnesota.

To set the record straight, these travels were not metaphorical, but seemed to be creatively and speculatively prudent. After all, the narrower tread-width of my 1961 Chevrolet Corvair (as documented in the owner's manual) was perceived in my worldview to be a perfect sidewalk fit. Plus, as time passed, I got into trouble about this only once, with Dave Benson, dean of men. Not a bad record.

As I drove down the sidewalk from a girl's dorm late one evening, Dave Benson shouted, "Jepson, pull off to the side of the sidewalk!" I did. I did not set the parking brake, for Moorhead is as flat as Mishawaka. I slowly got out of the vehicle and put my hands (properly, as I had seen on television cop shows with cases somewhat like this) on top of the car for frisking.

Meanwhile, the dean was walking slowly out of the dark night toward me. He stopped and said, "Go to your room." As I carefully turned the steering wheel slightly to the left to get back on the sidewalk, I drove slowly and carefully off. It was calming for me to hear laughter coming from his direction.

My friends to this day say, "For real you did this?"

That's the question. These drives on campus brought some new and parallel realities.

Some normal human reactions seemed to be missing from the myriads of students who mysteriously started to walk on the far-right side of the sidewalks, perhaps with a little edge-thinking as they glanced and listened.

5

Bumper Stickers

Sticker statements are specific representations of connections with whatever is out there, to mark that which the senses cannot assuredly claim, but important for the individual who purchases and then applies the sticker.

The clerk at Osco Drug responded to my question with kind of a strange look one day when I, dressed in my usual black clerical shirt with Roman white collar and just as black two-piece suit and black shoes and black shoestrings and black socks and black belt with a black wallet in my back pocket, asked him if they still had the *I Love Mishawaka, Indiana,* bumper stickers.

The employees of this drugstore, located in the shadow of the Golden Dome of the University of Notre Dame, often misperceived me to be a short Roman Catholic priest.

I imagine this clerk likely continues to wonder whether

that was a normal question of a perceived priest person who came into the store, wandered about a bit, and purchased no beer or Irish whiskey for a monastery.

That morning, during my food aisle wanderings and his wonderings, I did notice the beautiful portrayals of elegantly plated cream-style corn cans (including the very finest table settings) on labels including prominent name-brand logos, definitely intimidating the generic cans on the shelves below.

How powerful are these labels (and in some ways, "stickers") displaying to the world that which is not observable (i.e., the contents of the cans). Their representations are very fragile, for it is sad and somewhat unthinkable that many of even the elite labels will soon be rotting in a cemetery-like landfill. It's uncanny. But they, during their short shelf lives with exact expiration dates not unlike dates on tombstones, do promise so much! The promises include the aroma of cream-style corn filling kitchens across the land with long lines of people taking their places at the tables to experience the good life while helping the stalk market.

I do remember my dad talking about cream-style corn. He worked in a cannery when he was a Gustavus Adolphus College student. "Even then," he would say, "cream-style corn labels purported a product to be surely on a king's table." But my dad would always conclude his comments by saying, "You have no idea what was put in those cans. I do. I will never eat cream-style corn."

But enough of this corn. I was here for one purpose … to get an *I Love Mishawaka, Indiana,* bumper sticker.

The clerk responded, "They're in checkout lane two."

No one was checking there, so he pointed them out from lane one. All along I had assumed they would be displayed prominently, and that's why I had wandered around the store. But now it made sense. The stickers were appropriately stuck behind the scanning equipment and the tabloids.

My joy about their being there was reflected in my voice. "How much are they?"

He said, "Five cents."

"Really!" said I, as I went over to select one, at least the third from the front to avoid shop wear. This paralleled my rule that I have taught my wife Linda and daughter Abby, to always reach back at least three cans on shelves to avoid purchasing older, dented cans in favor of those that may be fresher and more elite looking.

I brought my selection over to him, handed him a dime, and felt satisfaction in receiving the receipt with a nickel change. Again, my face looked joyful, for I had expected a tax to be stuck on. It really was a good sticker price.

"Have a good day," he said. I felt a little surprised that he didn't wish me well, as most Mishawaka merchants do with the words, "Have a good day, Father."

Only two miles from home, I decided to head there along East Day Road (which is also open at night) to apply the sticker right away. After I drove the wagon halfway into the left side of our garage for the installation, I first spotted the bottle of professional cleaner, went over and took it off the shelf, sprayed down the rear bumper, and wiped it clean.

Very carefully I removed the backing from the sticker, lined it up perfectly, applied it, and stepped back and forth several times to see how great it looked on my 1987 Chevrolet Celebrity Eurosport station wagon. Sometimes the license branch person would look at the vehicle color box on the renewal form that reported *mahogany* and ask if I had a wooden wagon.

The sticker looked great, very much like an elite label. But in somewhat of a haunting way, I wondered why this sticker is so important. From a philosophical view, I also wondered if Mishawaka is out there.

Not unlike "Is there sound in the forest when a tree

falls when only deaf squirrels are present?" the question comes to be, "Will a Mishawaka sticker coming out of The Forest neighborhood be perceived in a radically different way on a treeless street in South Bend?"

Or perhaps this sticker statement as a specific representation is only that of another community "out there or even in there" like *Brigadoon* in Alan Jay Lerner's and Frederick Loewe's musical, the mysterious Scottish village that appears for only one day every one hundred years.

After all, the original "out there" crashing tree philosophical episode includes many assumptions that should be questioned, such as the belief that assumed apple trees grew and originally fell in the garden of Eden, for there is no sound, core evidence mentioned by Eve and Adam.

Sticker statements do indeed elicit interest about many externalities.

The too-soon death of the 1987 wagon occurred at the I-25 exit 219 in Denver with only 418,000+ miles on the odometer. It ended up with the *I Love Mishawaka, Indiana,* bumper sticker in a Colorado cemetery-like landfill. I also was crushed when this happened.

The new bumper came with an attached 1996

Oldsmobile Bravada, a fine vehicle purchased on February 4, 2008, with only 123,237 miles.

A bona fide Christian fish logo was stuck on the Bravada. It was scaled back a little.

The fish is a symbol of Christian identity, thought to have been chosen by the Christians for several reasons:

- The Greek word for fish (*ichthus*) comes to be an acrostic for "Jesus Christ, God's Son, Savior."
- The fish was early on not an obvious Christian symbol to persecutors.
- Jesus's ministry is associated with fish, for he chose several fishermen and made them fishers of people.
- Christian Lutheran Swedes and Norwegians love lutefisk.

The story goes that during the persecution of the early church, when a Christian would meet with someone new, she would draw a single arc in the sand. If the other person was a Christian, he would complete the sand drawing of the fish with a second arc. If not a Christian, the second person would not know the first was a Christian because of the ambiguity of the half-symbol.

My Bravada's scaled-back version included no *ichthus*, but instead *lutefisk*, a prized dish of those of us whose ancestries hearken back to the Nordic countries. The name literally means "lyefish." Even now, as my mouth excessively waters, I relate that lutefisk is made from aged fish carelessly dumped in lye, gelatinous in texture, giving off an extremely strong, pungent, and obnoxious odor.

I was one of the pastors at Calvary Lutheran Church in Alexandria, Minnesota, where hundreds and hundreds and hundreds of us devout Swedish Lutherans would annually in stoic silence wait in the church nave to have our numbers called to descend to the basement to devour this heavenly treat and then meditate expectantly about next year's feast, looking with side glances at attendees not of Nordic extraction who appeared somewhat disgusted and sick.

Added imagery is given in Garrison Keillor's book *Pontoon:*

Lutefisk is cod that has been dried in a lye solution. It looks like the dessicated cadavers of squirrels run over by trucks, but after it is soaked and reconstituted and the lye is washed out and it's cooked, it looks more fish-related, though with lutefisk, the window of success is small. It can be tasty but the statistics aren't on your side. It is the hereditary delicacy of Swedes and Norwegians who serve it around the holidays, in memory of the ancestors, who ate it because they were poor. Most lutefisk is not edible by normal people. It is reminiscent of the afterbirth of a dog or the world's largest chunk of phlegm (Keillor, 2007).

The second 1996 Bravada sticker, *Coexist*, had religious symbols resembling the letters that spell *coexist*. The sticker of choice reflects forty-plus years of my ecumenical and interreligious roles. This nonconformist belief sticker is an extension of my explorative connections, dismissing divisive rumors and naïve stances, not weighing who is assumed to be right and who is assumed to be wrong. It's about showing humanity's love grounded in God, supporting religious freedom and understanding that leads to peace.

My 1996 Bravada has been succeeded by a 2002 Bravada. There is presently no lutefisk bumper sticker. Instead, I sport a blue and yellow shirt with a large emblem that reads, "Lutefisk Lovers Association." The words on the back say, "I've Paid My Dues!"—a common Lutheran expression following the annual congregation budget meeting.

6

The Infinite Unknowns

As I have alluded before, an often-ignored consideration about daily life is that of the infinite unknowns. Infinitude is the quality or state of endlessness. As Albert Einstein put it, "Only two things are infinite, the universe and human stupidity, and I'm not sure about the former."

Basic to the philosophy of sense perception is to question how mental processes and symbols depend on the world internal and external to the perceiver.

Today, I can walk along the south side of East Lincolnway in Mishawaka and experience buildings on the north side labeled in concrete from the late 1800s, the world external. Years after the construction of these buildings, I was born a human being with internal senses. In the year of my birth, 1943, my perception of the external world began, generating empirical concepts representing the world around me within a mental framework connecting my perceptions to preexisting externals.

The big question is this: What are my unique discrepancies between the external world and my own neural processes producing perceptions determined by my 1943 wired brain, which started about eight o'clock in a morning that year in June? Do my perceptions allow me between the dates on my tombstone to perceive the external world as it really was, is, and will be by other human beings? Can I ever know of someone else's perceptions today or of those who have died or of those who will inhabit this globe one hundred years from now?

My personal internal perception of trees has always beckoned me. They sometimes stand alone and other times take their places in beautifully spaced communities, forested oases too large to explore totally, mirages of life with mist and rain, tall grasses and budding limbs and branches, a symphony of color with winds, storms, or fragrant breezes directed by the Creator. The protuberance of a node in late winter promising a place for a leaf is accompanied with other repetitions of the mysterious creation. Gardens take on a stronger scent of flowering trees and herbs as one seems to wander through them behind God as he encourages us to slow down and check out the lilies:

And why do you worry about clothing? Consider the lilies of the field, how they grow; they neither toil nor spin (Matthew 6:28).

When a personal perception is built on preexisting externals, that can be good stuff.

In the 1950s my cousin Alice and I would sit in the lifeless hulks of discarded autos and pickup trucks, hidden behind the chicken coop in the woods on her parents' farm in southwestern Minnesota. My sister Lenida and cousins Mary and Werner would never join us because they were too old.

I usually drove. We would enjoy those rare rides beside the ever-changing wildflowers and thistles framed by the out-buildings with peeling paint. My talent would also add a variety of mimicked engine sounds, and our conversations continued similar sounds and movements and topics of our relatives who drove these vehicles, silenced by death and rust.

Our family would leave the relatives' farms of cows, horses, dogs, John Deere Bs, uncles, aunts, and cousins to return home. Montevideo was another pleasant perception, a place with fabricated tree-lined streets and avenues.

The trees were planted well before 1943. In the 1950s, I perceived sidewalks rising in places from the unseen activity of aggressive roots searching for their God-given freedom.

In our backyard I prepared my first garden, spading up the small rectangular space and purposefully enriching the soil with fresh fish heads. This garden took on an appealing scent for several dogs from the neighborhood. After the dogs left, with renewed enthusiasm I hopefully planted seeds again and eventually viewed the silent process of growing vegetables from my tractor tire turned into a sandbox.

So, do our individual perceptions allow us between the dates on our tombstones to experience the world as it really was, is, and will be?

Perception is an awareness of what's going on as we walk or stand or drive or sit or play or plant. Sense perception is not only on philosophical agendas, but scientific ones as well, decade after decade, generation after generation.

The Mind/Body Connection

Who am I? Who are you? Who are we? We usually assume that our senses inform us about the world external, including our own bodies and the bodies around us.

Of course, when I think of my body, there seems to be an immediate distinction: I am my body; you are your body. With this distinction we can ask, "Where am I in my body? In my head, my arm, my foot?" Or if there is a question about this, we could say, "Perhaps I should look at my appendix for some supplementary possibilities."

In theological circles, human beings have sometimes been understood to be composed of two entities: a physical body and a spiritual soul, sometimes referred to as substance dualism.

There are challenges to this thinking. Historians suggest that substance dualism thinking about human composition made inroads into Christian thinking from Greek philosophy, not from scriptures.

Metaphysicians argue that the ability for the immaterial to interact with the material seems untenable. In scientific disciplines neuroscientists tend to indicate that consciousness is totally a physical occurrence.

Philosophers, scientists, and theologians have proposed monistic views of human composition over substance dualism, suggesting that humans are of one substance, physical.

The daily sense perception of my external body seems to be somewhat predictable and normal. As I adjust the telescoping mirror to the left of my left side vanity each morning to maintain and occasionally alter my sideburns or mustache, I am met with few surprises except on the days of entering new decades. It is amazing how ear and eyebrow and nose hairs spouted with birthdays fifty and sixty and how bumper crops needed to be cut down on the day I hit seventy with a new, sharp Bic razor and a more generous amount of lather.

My ritualistic observations in the mirror for some reason do not ignite much speculation as do many of my variable worldviews of reality. Perhaps this is partly due to a connection with not Bic's but Ockham's razor.

Ockham's razor is a principle attributed to fourteenth-century logician and Franciscan friar William of Ockham, native of this village in the English county of Surrey. The principle states, "Entities should not be multiplied unnecessarily."

Scientists have applied or reinvented Ockham's razor with sayings such as, "When you have two competing theories that make exactly the same predictions, the simpler one is better." Just take it at face value.

This is the philosophical version by Ernst Mach, called the principle of economy: "Scientists must use the simplest means of arriving at their results and exclude everything not perceived by the senses." This eventually becomes *positivism*: there is no difference between something that exists but is not observable and something that doesn't exist at all.

Bodily awareness has not been a huge topic for philosophers, with the notable exception of phenomenologists. Phenomenology (from Greek *phainomenon* "that which appears" and *logos* "study") is the philosophical study of the structures of experience and consciousness.

Phenomenology was founded in the early years of the twentieth century by Edmund Husserl. In its most basic form, phenomenology tries to create conditions for the objective study of topics normally regarded as subjective, including religious adherence. This is presented in chapter 13, "The Spectrum of Spiritualties and Phenomenology."

A good question cut out for us when we're curious about bodily awareness is, "Am I aware of my body as a trombonist in a pep band in the same way as I am perceptually aware of another person, such as the basketball player who just shot a three-pointer?"

One way to characterize the connection that we perceive only with our own bodies is to say that only our own bodies are perceived from the inside. In contrast, many bodies, including our own, can be perceived by us from the outside. This duality of access to our own bodies is known as the *touchant-touche* phenomenon. So as a trombonist in the pep band, when I hold the trombone with my hands, I have a tactile experience of the trombone from the outside *(touche)*, but I have also a tactile experience of the trombone from the inside *(touchant)*, which is also true of my hands. The same holds true with shaving and the brushing of teeth.

8

The Complexities of Identities and Edge-Thinking

Some mind/body connections seem fragile and short-lived, while others seem cosmically frozen. My personal identity in the community takes on a rather strange connection once a year, on Halloween.

I'll be sitting in a McDonald's in late October or in one of its archrivals, casually sipping some coffee—and a person will walk up and ask, "Where did you get your Nehru costume?" And then the very next day, a person will walk up and ask if I'm a priest. I, of course, tweak this more frozen, common, slight misinterpretation by saying, "I'm a Lutheran pastor, one of those people who first surfaced on Halloween some years ago." These perceived identities are to be expected, for the ways people present themselves not only impact the perceiver but the perceived.

Never will I forget the first time I donned my clerical collar at Northwestern Lutheran Theological Seminary in 1967. I could scarcely recognize myself in the mirror. I looked like a stranger with a mustache just like mine. I also felt that I would never escape this suspicious identity, for I had not only mistakenly used the long shank collar button in front instead of in back, almost choking myself and/or permanently destroying my Adam's apple, but could not remove it for forty-five minutes, receiving no response other than laughter from other seminarians. This episode was very meaningful, for it connected to my studies of the Hebrew Scriptures; a core reason why this projection at the front of the neck formed by the thyroid cartilage of the larynx is called the Adam's apple stems from the perception that a piece of the forbidden fruit became lodged in Adam's throat.

This fashionable, mysterious identity is elicited by the possibility that the collars worn by Roman Catholic priests and other Christian clergy may have roots with the mandarin collar that eventually came to be the collar of choice with the Nehru look, respecting India's first prime minister, Jawaharial Nehru. This look was popularized in the 1960s and 1970s with the minimalism of the Mod lifestyle, spread wide with the images of the Monkees and the Beatles. So in a way, the complexity of identities followed diverse trends of fashion running neck and neck.

Emerging and transformed identities reveal fashion's ability to radically change not only the ways we are perceived but also in the ways we perceive ourselves.

In her essay "Addressing the Body," Joanne Entwistle suggests that our perceived bodies constitute our environment, making them inseparable from self. She goes on to say that human identity is realized by dressed bodies. "Nakedness," she reveals, "is wholly inappropriate in almost all social situations and, even in situations where naked flesh is exposed (on the beach, at the swimming pool, even in the bedroom), the bodies that meet there are likely to be adorned, if only by jewelry, or indeed, even perfume: when asked what she wore to bed, Marilyn Monroe claimed that she wore only *Chanel No. 5*" (Entwistle, 2000).

Anthropologists seem to be in bed with this, saying that dress is a basic fabric of social life identity, that all people dress the body in some way with clothing, tattooing, cosmetics, body painting, plastic surgeries, haircuts, nose rings, mustaches, French berets, or even jars of creams promising to erase wrinkles.

Over the ages, identities of religious people have been locked in by standards for modesty, generally following the rule of Joanne Entwistle with an emphasis on dressed or covered bodies. Identity standards such as this, common in most world religions, seek to address the moral issues stemming from people's sexuality in society and in human interactions. Codes have always had a strong influence on some attitudes about modesty not only in dress but in behavior and speech as well.

But sure enough, as expected, there is a deep chasm separating individuals who confess religious adherence and perceptions. A natural example is called religious naturism (nudism). The following paragraphs expose this topic.

About 5.4 miles from our home in northern Indiana, there is a nudist recreation park with a lot of trees and leaves, founded in 1947. Others say it was confounded in 1947. I have read on their website that back there in the woods social and recreational centerpieces include a twenty-four-foot by fifty-foot heated swimming pool, a sauna, a hot tub, a deck for sunning and relaxing, volleyball, horseshoes, shuffleboard, table tennis, and the Toasted Buns Café. It's my assumption that all this is without an added cover charge.

We of the cloth and others may protest that individuals committed to a philosophy of naturism and nudism should come out of the woods and walk a new path. So, why would many (especially Lutheran pietists) say that these nudists are wearing many sins?

This call for confession and reform naturally would have been especially true for one such as I who grew up as a humble, perfect preacher's kid, well armored with strict moral codes of Swedish Lutheran pietism that were carried on stormy seas on the ships headed for Ellis Island and then to the new promised land called Minnesota. Once in the promised land, the undaunted magnetism of the blinding and numbing horizontal blizzards confirmed the belief that all pious Lutherans know what it is not to sin, to bundle up with many layers of clothing, well-covered and decent.

I continue to reflect in my genes two-thirds of what it is to be a humble, model Swede, which isn't too bad: blond, blue-eyed, and short. Perhaps my lack of height boldly reflects, and rightfully so, the nineteenth-century setting of the modernization of Sweden, a change from a righteous rural to a sin cities society and the putting down of some of my underprivileged rural class ancestors.

To detail this a bit, the programs of reform in Sweden were met with the discontent of the humble classes. Not to be put down even more, these Swedes decided shortly to check out a future someplace else in the cosmos, an immense space of challenging dreams where even proverbially strong mosquitos cannot survive unreal shivering springs.

It had been perceived in the Brigadoon-type villages tucked away in the ethereal prairies of Sweden that local Lutheran pastors were not taking enough time to drink coffee and munch cookies with matriarchs in congregations. Worse yet, since the church was supported by public taxation, it was rumored that the pastors were preoccupied with government reports and that they came across as anything but spiritual.

So, wouldn't you know, revivals were born. Also, in isolated, rural, small, and humble cottages the laity gathered to read the Bible. The meetings were at nightfall in cosmically stoic cottages with an overwhelming shyness as women and men gulped down gallons of coffee and munched on cookies, cakes, and barsss. The rooms were always hauntingly lighted dimly, for the setting sun was confined to the ethereal prairie behind drawn and musty drapes. A Norwegian elkhound could be heard barking in the distance across the border over in Norway.

Moravian missionaries eventually came to Sweden and were the ones who added to this movement the spirit of pietism. This included the emotional and subjective parts of the Christian experience plus the ethical and moral demands for those who wished to be a holy people. As this revivalism grew, so did the temperance movement, and many, hidden from public view in their cellars, drank to that.

Until 1820, however, there was no one to provide leadership for these changes. But suddenly, one appeared in the person of George Scott, an English Methodist missionary who set up his main office in Stockholm.

It's important to point out that Scott thought it was okay for all of his Swedish fan club to maintain the Lutheran identity, so long as they repented and possibly overhauled their bodies with Methodist adornments. Perhaps this could have included large but subdued "I like John Wesley" buttons and buggy stickers.

One loyal follower of Scott was Carl Olof Rosenius (1816–1868), a theological student at Uppsala University. In 1842, when Scott returned to England likely following a farewell reception with buns and minced ham, cake, pickles, green Jell-O laced with cottage cheese, gallons of coffee, Kool-Aid, barsss, and cookies, leadership was taken up by Rosenius.

Because the National Church of Sweden in the eyes of

Rosenius had fallen to a low estate, he refused ordination. Instead, he was a lay-evangelist for the rest of his life with a great love for the church and believed change in the church must come from within the church.

To encourage this, he published a newspaper, *Pietisten*, which pushed a rejection of the pleasures and standards of this world and an obedience to the divine injunction to be nice and perfect (Matthew 5:48). These themes were taken up in hymns composed by Mrs. C. O. Berg under her maiden name, Lina Sandell. It is amazing that my sister's name is Lenida Sandahl. The names could sound identical with a Swedish brogue.

Such, then, is part of the background leading to a new identity to the "I'm guilty but I can do better" lives of the frozen chosen growing up in Minnesota. In the Church of Sweden this development was compared to what Puritanism had been to the Church of England.

Although this pietism emphasized love for the national church for decades, this was not the end of the story. Humble people began to preach against Lutheran doctrines of the church and the sacraments, holding that the congregation be composed of the converted and saved and that the sacraments be reserved for only the converted worthy. Some rejected infant baptism.

One extreme separatist movement, the Eric Jansonites, came to America and founded a communistic colony in Bishop Hill, Illinois. My dad, Pastor Carl Jepson, served Immanuel Lutheran Church in neighboring Altona, Illinois, in the 1950s. The parishioners there were never called Jepsonites.

The rest of this story reveals that until 1880, the rural area of Sweden saw more than 5.5 times as many emigrants as any other social class. The free land policy in the United States drew these Swedish farmers. The most readily available land was in the upper Mississippi Valley, which came to be the heartland of the Augustana (Swedish) Lutheran Church.

It is true that many of these immigrants were, as in Sweden, not interested in religion. Some were even hostile toward the church, for in Sweden they had seen the church siding with the status quo. These separatists were not interested in an institution reminding them of the church back home, so they either went to places like Bishop Hill or became Methodists or Baptists.

In 1870, of the ninety-seven thousand Swedish Nationals in the United States, only nineteen thousand identified with the Augustana Lutheran Church. These were the right-wing dissenters, the faithful Old Lutherans.

Their Swedish Lutheran pietism was actually on some of the same pages with other religious traditions. The Amish women, who also love Mishawaka, Indiana, mirror Swedish Lutheran pietistic women (whose shadows in the upper Midwest are fading) with the avoidance of lipstick and other makeup.

We Swedish Lutheran preachers' kids had a favorite tract, predominantly placed in the tract rack in the church narthexes. It was titled, "Dance Your Way to Hell." It really felt fine to read all four pages of this publication and then go to school and watch those unfortunate kids on the dance floor on their way.

This righteous identity carried over into my college years when I was a trombonist in a dance band at Concordia College. Our performances were quite fine, and the stoic Norwegian-type listeners sitting (dancing not permitted) in the Normandy Room really enjoyed our talents.

Some of these pietistic lifestyles parallel those of the Shakers. The Shakers, who do not have sex, were outdone by Lutheran pietism with the teaching that there isn't such a thing as sex. For years I was amazed by how babies were found in hospitals and then taken home.

So how do I now view my pious upbringing? I can

say that it was great, for it helped and encouraged me to become curious.

So it becomes curious to ask, dressed in Sunday's best, if there can actually be religious naturism. In fact, religious nudists are parts of many religious bodies.

They, for example, find no conflict between the teachings of the Bible and the ways they live their lives and worship without clothing, believing that covering the body leads to sexualization, a fine-tuning of fashion design that leads to identities that allure or charm or entice or tempt.

Religious naturists believe that there have been misinterpretations of the events portrayed in the garden of Eden story and the fall. They believe that the common notion that nudity and sexualization go hand in hand is a worldly, naïve point of view.

Their optional view of the garden of Eden story and the fall goes like this:

- Genesis 2:25: "And the man and his wife were both naked, and were not ashamed." This means that they were blameless because they were created naked by God. They designed fig leaves after eating the forbidden fruit. Soon they were hiding behind trees and leaves in the woods.

- When confronted by God, with the fig leaves in place, Adam says they're hiding because of nakedness. "(God) said, 'Who told you that you were naked?'" (Genesis 3:11a).

- Since there were no other human beings, religious naturists believe it was the devil who told Adam and Eve that they were naked. Their belief is that God was displeased by their eating of the forbidden fruit, but also displeased with their attempt to cover up their bodies.

- Religious naturists say the definition of the human body is separate, distinct, and nonmaterialistic. They believe that the human body was God's final and the most wonderful earthly creation. To require the body to be covered is seen as legalism. In fact, this view says that many people have been deceived into thinking that clothing keeps them from sinning when the opposite is true.

These various ravines that separate all of us have been dug with interpretations of scriptures and formulations of doctrines becoming ideologies (i.e., prescriptive dualistic proclamations without the support of rational arguments that promote personal interests at the expense of someone else's). All too often the truth that we impose as divinely revealed is really our own disguised subconscious will to maintain the status quo or to protect superiority.

My ecumenical and interreligious leadership roles echo the line of reasoning portrayed by Paul Knitter. He reminds us that philosophers urge philosophical maturity, which demands that we accept that all knowledge is theory-laden—for each society has a different plausibility structure, and each religion speaks within its own language game.

This ploy, Knitter purports, is centered within the struggle for liberation and justice with the activity of believers from different traditions instead of being intent on searching for "one God" or "one Ultimate" or a "common essence" or a "mystical center." He says that appropriate, diverse traditions *can* experience together "that which grounds their resolves, inspires their hopes, and guides their actions to overcome injustice and to promote unity" (Knitter, 1988).

Theologian Harvey Cox summarizes this thinking by saying, "Interfaith dialogue becomes neither an end in itself nor a strictly religious quest, but a step in anticipation of God's justice. It becomes praxis. Similarities and differences which once seemed important fade away as the real differences between those whose sacred stories are used to perpetuate domination and those whose religion strengthens them for the fight against domination— emerge more clearly" (Cox, 1985).

This image of a deep chasm is multiplied innumerable times. A document entitled "Our Mission and Inter-Religious Dialogue" of the Thirty-Fourth General Congregation of the Jesuits, held in 1995, begins:

If we imagine, as Ignatius did, the Trinity looking down on the earth as the third millennium of Christianity is about to unfold, what would he see? More than five billion human beings—some male, some female; some rich, many more poor; some yellow, some brown, some black, some white; some at peace, some at war; some Christian (1.9 billion), some Muslim (1 billion), some Hindu (777 million), some Buddhist (341 million), some of new religious movements (128 million), some of indigenous religions (99 million), some Jewish (14 million), some of no religion at all (1.1 billion).

A quest comes to be for how we respond to the racism, cultural prejudice, religious fundamentalism, and intolerance that mark what some call *reality*.

9

The Limited Scope of Ancient Cosmological Stories

The older version of Genesis starting at 2:4, which was finally penned in the tenth century BC, has the emphasis on people tending and tilling the earth and eating a lot of something. I'm not going to say apples, for a philosophy of perception by these folk is missing.

> *The Lord God took the man and put him in the garden of Eden to till it and keep it. And the Lord God commanded the man, "You may freely eat of every tree of the garden; but of the tree of the knowledge of good and evil you shall not eat, for in the day that you eat of it you shall die." (Genesis 2:15-17)*

The newer version of Genesis, likely from the sixth century BC, posits the birth of the entire cosmos. A problem with this version is that it is at odds with modern scientific knowledge, including the presence of light before the creation of the sun.

> *Then God said, "Let there be light"; and there was light. And God saw that the light was good; and God separated the light from the darkness. God called the light Day, and the darkness he called Night. And there was evening and there was morning, the first day. (Genesis 1:3–5)*
>
> *God made the two great lights—the greater light to rule the day and the lesser light to rule the night—and the stars. God set them in the dome of the sky to give light upon the earth, to rule over the day and over the night, and to separate the light from the darkness. And God saw that it was good. And there was evening and there was morning, the fourth day. (Genesis 1:16–19)*

The conclusion, then, is that the authors of both versions did not have a huge concern about cosmology, even admitting that human reason cannot comprehend anything so mysterious as the creation and (second) the structuring of the cosmos. In defense of other possible explanations, the presence of light before the creation of the sun could be based on the belief that God is the light of the world.

The Bible was formatted over many centuries, involving many authors and reflecting shifting patterns of religious belief.

A very small segment of the ancient Israelite community contributed to the writings. It's interesting to note how beliefs are maintained by communities, built on layers and becoming connected.

A contribution of the ancient Israelites submitted the universe to be made up of a flat disc-shaped earth floating on water with heaven above, underworld below. Human beings were on earth during life and in the underworld after death, a morally neutral location. In Hellenistic times, Jews began to connect to the Greek idea that the underworld was a place of punishment and that righteous people would enjoy the afterlife in heaven.

The first chapter of Genesis containing a summary of how the cosmos originated says that Yahweh, the God of Israel, was totally responsible for creation with no rivals. Later on, Jewish thinkers, connecting to Greek philosophy, came to promote that God's wisdom, word, and spirit penetrated all things, which gave them unity. Christianity eventually connected to these beliefs and identified Jesus as the creative word.

Here is the surprise!

As mentioned, ancient writers did not have a huge concern about cosmology. But this lack of interest did not continue in centuries that followed. Instead, there came to be an *acceptance* of these speculations, labeling them as literally true. This led to their becoming articles of faith in order to demean beliefs and traditions that reflected the observing and reasonable but pagan philosophers, including Plato and Aristotle.

A snaillike process of education did lazily gain acceptance, leading to the twelfth century, when the Genesis picture of water held above the firmament to protect the earth from devastation by celestial fire was challenged as irrational. Then in the thirteenth century, the submerged theories of Aristotle surfaced and were soon affirmed by the church, becoming a centerpiece of philosophic training in Christian learning for the next four hundred years.

Philosopher Thomas Aquinas, of the theology department at the University of Paris, along with Albertus

Magnus and Roger Bacon, were successful in bringing classical science as an ally of scriptural cosmology. These scholastics emphasized that reason is appropriate for legitimizing the truth of scriptures. Aquinas went even further to say that scientific knowledge and biblical doctrine issue from the same source.

It was Aquinas who ended the debate over Aristotelian cosmology, allowing universal appeal for Aristotle's model of the universe, with an earth center including numerous celestial spheres. It was suggested that the motions of these spheres were controlled by separate intelligences, agreeing with Aquinas's view that angels, divinely controlled, moved the heavenly bodies. Add to this a defined differentiation between the perfect, eternal matter of the heavens and the imperfect, transitory matter of earth.

This cosmology came to be accepted as an accurate picture of the physical universe; the connection between the heavens and the earth provided celestial bodies to affect material events, a conduit for God to work his will.

Some snail speed remained. But the huge benchmark of 1543 of the Polish astronomer Copernicus eventually shifted Christian cosmology to accommodate the discovery that the earth revolves around the sun. Eventually.

Christian cosmology denied the Copernican theory for two hundred years!

In our contemporary experience, the religious world more and more depends on astronomers and physicists than on theologians for understandings of the cosmos. Religion's cosmological stories are now generally treasured as poetic or symbolic.

At the same time, physicists do position at least a portion of the Genesis version of the creation as scientifically quite plausible. This big bang theory comes from evidence that the universe was born at a definite, creative moment. A fairly popular theological insight also connects with naming the big bang as the first incarnation of God. This is presented further in chapter 14, "The Cosmic Christ and the First Incarnation?"

Of course, some individuals continue to insist that scientific truth is hidden in the sacred pages of the Bible, to be eventually revealed.

10

Beliefs and Societal Changes

Beliefs are contextual. If a community's context refuses to consider societal changes, its culture and beliefs remain in some ways commendable but isolated, dualistic, and possibly even naïve.

Times have changed. Societies have been given new shapes in pluralistic global cultures. In contrast, the apostolic faith for some remains with a solid, frozen, and comatose presence. From my experience, many northern Lutherans (including me) would sit next to each other in cold pews in small churches with wood stoves and more or less believe in what they had always heard.

It has been suggested that belief today may be in one holy catholic digitized religious institution. This is a thesis of an article by Brigham Young University law school professor Frederick Mark Gedicks writing with

Roger Hendrix. Their article showcases the revolutionizing instant digital reproduction of almost any images or words, without limitations, for anyone anywhere, which produces new markets. This, the article continues, explains the present passion for just purchasing some spirituality, making possible God himself to be unattached to traditions (Gedicks and Hendrix, 2005).

This balmy, sophisticated digitized climate grows innumerable versions of less-judgmental, less-demanding spirituality. This shopping cart religion calls people to assemble collections of spiritual beliefs that are beautifully packaged, instant but not frozen, satisfying for the moment. Sometimes the image of the cross-migraine and the implied unbelievable servanthood prescribes instant pain relief and new massages.

Massages. I'm showing my age as I hearken back to the days of being a devotee to Marshall McLuhan and having conversations with his associate, Barrington Nevitt.

McLuhan was a Canadian professor and philosopher. His ideas are viewed as cornerstones of the study of media theory.

He became identified with the phrase, "The medium is the massage." He proposed that a medium itself, such as television or film, shapes and controls the scale and form of human association and action.

I personally look back to those enlightening years of the early 1970s with the study of communication theory. There was talk in our classes of the dangers of a consumerist society in *the electric age* as McLuhan probed into ideas surrounding the impact of mass communication. Imagine a half century ago McLuhan said that in a consumerist society, the development of technology can cause us to be extensions of it instead of technology being an extension of us!

It follows that Gedicks introduced some of Charles Trueheart's predictions about the next church movement, one with "No spires. No robes. No clerical collars. (So I ask, no Nehru costumes?) No hard pews. No kneelers. No Biblical gobbledygook. No prayerly rote. No fire, no brimstone. No pipe organs. No dreary eighteenth-century hymns. No forced solemnity. No Sunday finery. No collection plates" (Trueheart, 1996).

The question comes to be that of the place of the finite—that is, having definite or definable limits, living a limited existence. We tend to be enamored with the finite and trust it. Some people avoid the generic cans, because the images of the major brands promise so much. I mean, what could be better than having shelves in our households stocked with packages of celestial teas leading to comfortable consciousness.

In the context of changing societies, the creative catalyst for me is to be cautiously open to cutting edge settings in the discipline(s) I passionately understand and love. The stages for innovative action are already behind the curtains, with various sets representing explosive changes in the world with philosophical, scientific, social, and theological resources that have been mysteriously lurking in the shadows from the beginning.

A label to attach to this mind-set is radical openness.

I don't feel uncomfortable or feel someone is out to get me when I admit I am radically open. I don't fear that my photo will be posted on a wall of the post office, although my photo on my driver's license would not look out of place in that location. I don't have nightmares of a Lutheran bishop tearing and ripping off my clerical collar. Instead, radical openness for me is a key for leading a happier, healthier life.

In 2007, a survey of more than ten thousand people from forty-eight countries, published in *Perspectives on Psychological Sciences*, revealed that happiness was viewed as more important than success, intelligence, knowledge, maturity, wisdom, relationships, wealth, and meaning in life.

Dr. Todd Kashdan, scientist, public speaker, and professor of psychology, says that one of the most reliable and overlooked keys to happiness is cultivating and exercising our innate sense of curiosity. Curiosity creates an openness to unfamiliar experiences that builds foundations for greater opportunities to experience discovery, joy, and delight. He points out that the majority of Americans spend most of their time and energy commuting, standing in line at the post office, fixing broken appliances, watching TV, snacking, or hanging out.

He offers the flip side, the benefits of curiosity: "Curiosity, at its core, is all about noticing and being drawn to things we find interesting. It's about recognizing and seizing the pleasures that novel experiences offer us, and finding novelty and meaning even in experiences that are familiar. When we are curious, we see things differently; we use our powers of observation more fully. We sense what is happening in the present moment, taking note of what is, regardless of what it looked like before or what we might have expected it to be" (Kashdan, 2009).

11

Worldviews and Radical Openness

One's view of the world can be conditioned with radical openness, the imaginative ability to form new images and sensations that go beyond that which is assumedly revealed through the senses. It is a cycle of image formation that is hidden, for it takes place without anyone else's knowledge.

A worldview is a psychological lens/filter that is revealed by the ways we perceive the world and act in it. Worldviews eventually can come to be belief systems promoting preferential views about God, life, the cosmos, or the pluses of a Studebaker rather than a Chevrolet. Worldviews can also be foundations for living life as a stoic Swede or a class clown. Sometimes worldviews are not intentionally chosen but instead are simply unique perceptions.

My worldview of department store escalators always moved me when I was extremely young. I loved riding them in Dayton's and Donaldson's in Minneapolis, but I could not understand how the stairs could move on so quickly and then others be manufactured immediately somewhere in a subbasement to replace them. In a similarly puzzled way, I remember at age 4.1 staring into the back of the radio in Brunswick, Minnesota, looking for small people playing tiny instruments in an orchestra. I preferred riding the roads constructed of concrete, for I loved Fig Newtons—convinced that the filling between the two lanes was that delicious fig paste. It was surprising to find out the FTD means Florists Transworld Delivery—so I quit looking for the wired flowers traveling along rural telephone lines. My view of parking meters expired when I noticed coins being retrieved by city employees into large money bags. Gone were the times when I envisioned the pennies, nickels, and dimes plummeting forever into the depths.

These somewhat unique worldviews of mine have not stopped. I believe this is fortunate; others don't.

When walking down the street in Jeffersonville, Indiana, one day when I was forty-four, I noticed freshly painted yellow metal boxes, one to a block. Each box had the words, "Fine Box." My worldview did not translate that they were related to expired parking meters. I commented to my friends, "Yes, they are. They really look fine." Laughter followed. And only a short time ago I was boarding a Delta flight, seat assignment in hand. I asked the flight attendant, "Do you need to wear glasses?" She said, "No … Why?" I responded, "Because I'm in 3D." Again, good laughter as we flew away.

To this day I stop by a kiosk in the University Park Mall that has a sign, "Watch Battery Experts." I stay for just a few moments because the experts just stand there.

I also perceive trips to the Walgreen's pharmacy to be rather dauntingly dangerous, for a sign above the right window with large letters says, "*Drop Off.*" As I speak with the pharmacist, I tend to make sure I'm on level ground as I wonder if the pharmacist is safe back there.

Another confusing and possibly dangerous area is often displayed on the swinging doors at the post office. One is marked *Out*, the other *In*. I wonder if these are directives for the persons going in to the outside or for me going out of the outside.

On McKinley Highway in Mishawaka there is a sign, "*No Passing School Zone.*" I wonder if many of the students are in their eighties or even nineties. It's a little embarrassing that I was in my sixties when I finally realized what the large object is on signs for Shell gas stations. It's a shell.

My personal, genetic worldviews do find some roots

in those of my dad, Carl W. Jepson, whose mind reached out in diverse and encompassing ways. He envisioned a bobsled and built one. Our first trip found us speeding down a steep, snowy hill behind the old library, a route never chosen before by other worldviews. Our worldview forgot about the twelve-foot concrete retaining wall at the bottom. Our speeding, innovative bobsled/plane may not have been the best, but it was a runner-up.

There are both personal and collective (consensual) worldviews.

- Some personal worldviews are *transformative*. These include mystical experiences or those that follow life events, such as marriage or parenthood.
- Collective (consensual) worldviews often validate personal worldviews (Studebaker or Mustang clubs).

My worldview at times includes an interplay flip of the collective (consensual) with the personal.

Early on in life, I did experience the collective September joy with others as we rushed down to Peterson Brothers Studebaker, relishing the new year looks of the Studebaker Hawks and Presidents. But my personal worldview expanded with my profound talent to mimic the sounds of not only Studebakers but also 1939 Chevrolets with vacuum shifting transmissions, 1951 Buicks, which I mimicked with their starting problems because of flooding carburetors due to the location of the starters *under* the accelerators, Greyhound buses, diverse trucks with air brakes, and John Deere B tractors pulling manure spreaders.

This personal worldview of being a person/engine eventually spread to my widely known fictitious occupation of being a dealer for the Maytag Diesel Pipe Organ Company. I, of course, being a person/engine, was able to provide on-sight demonstrations of the organs. As many years passed, wet-behind-the-ears pastors who did not have a full account of my deceptive but convincing sales ploys would ask for brochures to be shared back home with music committees.

Indeed, these talents drew interest. Girls and once in a while guys at Concordia College would kind of beg me to share my exhaustive performances with their friends. It was not uncommon in the cafeteria to hear, "Please, Leonard, *be* a 1939 Chevrolet for Diane."

This attraction, as is the case for most profound personal worldviews, is due to the fact that the majority of our society does not proudly develop personal inconsistencies. Instead, people for the most part are taught about worldviews that are presented as all-embracing and unambiguous descriptions of reality.

12

Mysticism and Radical Openness

Collective worldviews are very common, for they are generally imposed by specific societies and dominant religions and are consistently reinforced by immediate families, communities, and peers. Deviations from these socially accepted worldviews are often met with frowns.

Personal worldviews, in contrast, can be connected to people who are free-spirited or even classified as mystics. For mystics, the world is expansive and magical. Mystics' worldviews steer away from strict doctrines and principles. Their minds are open to haunting questions accompanied by a natural curiosity about the physical and spiritual world. They embrace a connection to every living thing and therefore can look beyond what may be socially accepted. They acknowledge that the cosmos is infinite and mysterious and is far too complex for the human mind to fully comprehend. Sometimes they are told to go to their rooms.

One day in seminary President Clemons Zeidler said, "Jepson, you are the only student mystic at Northwestern Lutheran Theological Seminary." A few days later, Professor Mark Hillmer told me to come into his office. I consented. It was déjà vu, so like being told to go to the coatroom.

After I entered Hillmer's inner sanctum with a little fear, I sat down. Professor Hillmer began. "I called you in today because I have observed that you have a very unique homiletical style. When you give sermons, the sentence structure is backward."

As I attempted to think the best about being backward, I said, "Right that is?"

"Yes," he continued. "And that's good—because you draw people into listening because of this very unusual way of communicating. It's very nice and weird."

"Two clue this is," thought I, "that a mystic am I?

"Well," pondered I, "when I work on a sermon, I do find myself taking the theme and imagining that topic isolated in space, without limitations. Out there in space, the theme grows, free of being infringed by any other. So, would this be why my sentences become creatively backward as thoughts return to the seminary and crash down mysteriously backward onto the keys of my 1961 Royal portable typewriter with brown carrying case?"

I really didn't want to be trapped into being a religious mystic. I don't even use Halo shampoo. This seemed to be very limiting for me, for my being is much more diverse than simply being mystical. I preferred people saying, "Jepson, you don't seem to be very religious." This always opened doors for speculation.

It allowed me to respond, "Thank you for the compliment. I will look further into this."

After all, I've always enjoyed being interactive and curious, encouraging without limiting others, to be inductive instead of being gripped with the rigidity of too much deductive thinking. If destined to be a mystic, I would miss mingling with ordinary, down-to-earth people. And likely my top-notch identity as an unusually humorous short guy would shrink with people pointing and saying disrespectfully, "Look at that funny, short mystic."

So, what can be a mystic? For a starter, a mystic generally is one who believes in the existence of realities beyond human comprehension, perhaps employing devout contemplation.

The description of author Matthew Fox has come to be most fitting for me.

I like his description because I'm not a fundamentalist and liberally liberal. Fox says, "Fundamentalism by definition is anti-mystical or distorts mysticism, and (also) much of liberal theology and religion is so academic and left-brained that it numbs and ignores the right brain which is our mystical brain. Seminaries teach few practices to access our mysticism. This is why many find religion so boring—it lacks the adventure and inner exploration that our souls yearn for. As St. John of the Cross said, 'Launch out into the deep'" (Fox, 2011).

This description is very comfortable for me. I've discovered that I'm a friendly, mild mystic who travels heuristically. Even though I enjoy crawling around the crawl space under our house to check for plumbing leaks, people will not think I'm a thoroughgoing mystic who lives somewhere in a sub–crawl space.

My radical openness to mystery in the realm of religion is demonstrated in part by a thesis put forth by Beverly J. Lanzetta. Her track travels to a theology of humility sensitive to religious pluralism. It is called apophatic (negative) theology, which attempts to describe God by negation, speaking only in terms of what may *not* be said about God. This is a discipline that focuses on a spontaneous, open experience of the divine beyond the realm of ordinary perception, often unmediated by traditional organized religion, conditioned role-playing, and learned defensive behavior (Lanzetta, 2001).

To say the least, worldviews are complex intellectual phenomena.

- On the *inclusive* level, they are a system of generalized views of the world and the place of humanity in it.

- A worldview commonly is also *individualistic*. A person becomes an individual with his/her formation of a community worldview. It is then when common people are able to speak of the held principles of their specific social group, social class, or party.

- From this point, an individualistic worldview can embrace *radical openness* to a range of expanded curiosities (i.e., *personal worldviews*), including questions such as the following:
    o What is the world that exists outside us?
    o What is the relationship between mind and matter?
    o What is a human being?
    o How do people come to know reality?

13

The Spectrum of Spiritualities and Phenomenology

For over two millennia, a Christian reflection about God joined and was given form by other more ancient faith traditions in articulating patterns of faith in God. Global speculations and affirmations about God continue to be abundantly confessed. There are other emerging spirituality movements and polarizations as well. The phenomenological method develops an empathetic understanding of the rich complexity of phenomena.

From my open, Christian perspective, I am well convinced that there has never been an "in a nutshell" Christian doctrine of God. Christian affirmations have been intentionally interwoven with other traditions and disciplines. This is a major reason behind my passion for ecumenical and interreligious involvements.

The very foundation and necessity for religious dialogue is built on the pluralities of heritages, including political, social, cultural, scientific, and philosophical. The complex historical developments of all religions reflect the mysteries of human existence.

As a parish pastor, I came to understand that exploration invites new perceptions; new perceptions can lead to changes with wider or narrower parameters; wider parameters present possibilities for listening; listening respects people and traditions of diverse backgrounds.

This was confirmed in nature in the prayer gardens at First English Lutheran Church. Each year we perceived the changes. Almost without notice, new environments surprisingly appeared through the senses. The rows of tall tomato plants would be gone, as were the sunflowers. But as one walked the twisting paths in late October, new sounds of the large, drying leaves of the tulip poplar tree were heard, blown by a gusty wind, accompanied by the deep tones of the large wind chimes.

Soon after late October 1517, there was a call to celebrate change, unfortunately with some narrower parameters. The Lutheran Victory Reformation, perhaps to be compared to some small Lutheran university defeating the University of Notre Dame inside the football stadium on a comfortable fall afternoon, would be followed with the postgame mass in the Basilica of the Sacred Heart as Lutheran fans smugly drove back home to Minnesota, stopping for coffee and lutefisk in Wisconsin.

These competitive games have changed somewhat. On October 31, 1999, Lutherans and Roman Catholics signed the Joint Declaration on the Doctrine of Justification, agreeing on the basic nature of the gospel, countering the divisions of the warring players.

Even though responses to Martin Luther and other reformers were slow, the Council of Trent (1545–1563) did articulate some new directions, eventually bringing the Counter-Reformation era to a more spiritual, more literate, and more educated level. Also, the Reformation's positive repercussions came to be seen in the intellectual and cultural emphases inspired on all sides of the schism.

What about other world religions?

Oral tradition communicates that St. Francis of Assisi made at least two explorations to Egypt to meet with the sultan, Melek al-Kamil, during the Christian crusades of the thirteenth century. The story recounts that one of the friars found a copy of the Koran and asked what he should do with it. Francis's reply was that if he would have found a single page of the Koran, he would have kissed it and placed it on the altar, because it was also written in love of God.

As Francis modeled, in the character of the Cosmic Christ, we are to welcome and encounter the stranger. This is discussed in chapter 14, "The Cosmic Christ and the First Incarnation?"

The heart of this ongoing exploration provides an antidote for people and communities who suffer from moods of disinterest, isolation, and ignorance. I like to call this exploration *spiritual formation*, not to be confined to religion.

Spiritual formation is a universal experience. It includes everyone, for it is the formation, be it good or bad, of character.

Terrorists, monks, young people, the retired, and those with special needs constantly portray spiritual formation. It is America's and every culture's greatest resource or greatest liability.

The American culture is becoming more secular. Statistics have confirmed that 25 percent of young adults in America, those born after 1980, characterize themselves religiously as atheist, agnostic, or "nothing in particular"— the *nones*. This is not necessarily dismal.

Author Robert C. Fuller says that the unchurched

spiritual seekers focus on inner sources of spirituality and on this world rather than the afterlife, for religion isn't a fixed thing. "Spirituality exists wherever we struggle with the issues of how our lives fit into the greater cosmic scheme of things" ... where the universe comes from, why we are here, or what happens when we die (Fuller, 2001).

Related to this quest identified by Fuller, Good Friday, which presently has less drawing power than Black Friday, speaks of life's mysteries and fatalities.

I submit that *fatal* is a deadly word. Later in life we think about it more. How will I die? When will that be? Where will I die? If I know I am dying, how will I react?

These questions even made a grown man cry: "Father, if you are willing, remove this cup from me; yet, not my will but yours be done" (Luke 22:42).

Some will simply eat, drink, and be merry and dismiss this concern. But let's consider this other path, spiritual formation, ancient among religions and philosophies.

This is a good point to introduce an expanded description of phenomenology.

Phenomenology is a philosophy or method of inquiry based on the premise that reality consists of objects and events as they are perceived or understood in human consciousness and not of anything independent of human consciousness.

Phenomenologists, be they philosophical, psychological, sociological, or theological, study individuals' awareness of the manifestations of life, how they express that awareness and how these expressions can be best understood.

Phenomenology was coined as a term in 1764 by the Swiss German mathematician and philosopher Johann Heinrich Lambert. The term referred to the illusory nature of human experience to attempt to develop a theory of knowledge about these experiences.

In the early 1900s, a series of studies on phenomenology was published by a German group. The most influential among the group was the Austrian-born philosopher Edmund Husseri. He and other phenomenologists generally reacted against a scientific methodology that demanded that life experiences be discarded for objective empiricism, the practice of relying on observation and experiment primarily in the natural sciences for verification. They called for a recognition that such experiences could be used as a means through which reality could be explored. Phenomenological methods now tout that nonempirical investigation is an appropriate tool for understanding fundamental realities of existence. Some philosophical phenomenologists have devoted themselves to the study of the phenomenology of religion.

A grand characteristic of the phenomenological method for ecumenical and interreligious studies of religions is that it does not seek to list or describe similar practices across diverse religious traditions in order to rate them from best to worst. In other words, phenomenologists develop a genuine empathetic understanding of the experiences in question. The phenomenological approach to the study of religion encourages the development of an empathetic understanding of the rich complexity of religious phenomena. Radical openness is the key for opening new understandings of religious phenomena in multiple contexts.

A good example of the power of radical openness can be realized with an empathetic understanding of a spiritual formation called a cosmic sympathy for the entire creation. Many of the ministries I have been connected to have been under the umbrella of the OFM, Order of Friars Minor, which reflects this cosmic sympathy built on the lifestyle of St. Francis of Assisi.

There was something weird about St. Francis and St. Claire, his female counterpart. Neither of them looked forward to hanging out on weekends. They had little interest in visiting local eateries or even considering new or more fashionable habits. Instead, they would spend whole weekends in tears. They would cry together. This spiritual formation provides a foundation for benevolence instead of self-absorption. It also teaches that humanity cannot fix everything.

The phenomenological method can also foster one's appreciation for a character of Christian mystics. They teach that the great teacher is darkness, not light. Darkness leads to faith instead of a fabrication of simple, hollow answers that we think can bring light … for a while. In other words, from a Christian perspective, this formation calls one to follow the Christ on the cross instead of worshiping him from a comfortable, lighted, and safe distance. The crucified one is an image of the invisible God who is on our side, involved with the way the cosmos is. In the Christ, God comes to identify with the pain of the whole world, to enter into it, and to invite us into that identification with sadness. This spiritual formation brings community to remain as far as possible on the edge, reaching out to others instead of eating, drinking, and making merry.

The mystery of tears, the mystery of sadness brings us into a different consciousness of God's creation:

I have said these things to you so that my joy may be in you, and that your joy may be complete. "This is my commandment, that you love one another as I have loved you. No one has greater love than this, to lay down one's life for one's friends." (John 15:11–13)

These mysteries are tied to my appreciation for the Franciscan Order's alternative view of atonement.

The English word for atonement originally meant *at-one-ment* or *at one with*, being in harmony with someone or in harmony with God.

The traditional atonement theology is portrayed in this way:

> *Jesus - died - for our sins.*
> —*Burma Shave*

When one thinks about this while driving down the road, this portrayal may appear like a *transaction*, with God loving the world because his Son is killed, as if God's love had to be purchased.

The Franciscan Order's alternative atonement theology is portrayed in this way:

God's love always has and always will come without conditions. No deal is required.

In the Christology of Franciscan Fr. Richard Rohr, he says that Jesus *let go* (died to) of the false self so there can be a birth of the true self (universal self) to be emulated by his followers.

This alternative understanding of the atonement has been with the Franciscans from their inception. The thirteenth century in the church was quite broadminded, and minority positions such as this were permitted.

14

The Cosmic Christ and the First Incarnation?

Each year the sudden, cold winds of late October and then November freeze into place those mystifying themes of Advent: the coming of the Christ at Christmas, the coming of the Christ into our lives today, and the coming of the Christ at the end of time. This extravagant, gigantic belief was meant to say that God will reign in the whole cosmos.

After the fourth century, the Western church opted to leave this cosmic, *inclusive* imagery of "the last things" for a less-awesome one that encouraged people to casually take on *individualized* plans. More modest and egocentric, these plans came to include descriptions such as "You will be able to enjoy looking down from heaven to check out what's going on after you leave earth down there," which can be used in obituaries. These plans eventually came to emulate a "build a pizza your own way" approach, imaging a simpler, homey approach to life beyond death.

This took the preparation punch out of Advent, so people started to think that they simply had to prepare the Christmas punch.

When the Western church did seem to abandon the inclusive imagery of "the last things," the real news of Advent lost touch with the belief that the whole creation is being reconstructed by God, that it is God's intention to make all things new, without exception. This is hard news to take when technology is making all things new, experiencing giant strides and promising so much for an electronic Christmas. On the other hand, God is acting! This is great news for people who are living in stables.

Contemporary theological writings about the Cosmic Christ, or world-Christ, call for a return to a cosmic, inclusive imagery. These writings suggest that in the holy scriptures the Christ's presence is proclaimed and counted in billions of years. The prologue to John's gospel, letters of Paul to Colossians and Ephesians, and the opening of John's first letter all speak of the Christ existing from all eternity.

It is with overwhelming depth that we can consider the Cosmic Christ because of the life and writings of Raimon Panikkar.

Panikkar died on August 26, 2010, at age ninety-one in a village near Barcelona. He was a key figure in the development of interreligious dialogue in the twentieth century.

His father, an upper-caste Hindu, was active in the movement against British rule in India. He was forced to flee from India and settled in Spain where he married Raimon's mother, a Catalan woman.

Raimon received a Catholic education in Barcelona. He was ordained a priest, studied at various universities, and received a doctorate in theology in 1961 from the Lateran University in Rome.

His life had taken a decisive turn in 1954 when he visited India for the first time. He encountered a group of Catholic monks in Varanasi who tried to express their Christianity by living as much as possible like Hindu ascetics. He was overwhelmed by the rich world of religion in India. For the rest of his life, the example of these monks encouraged him to integrate their world with his Christian faith.

Panikkar's first book, *The Unknown Christ of Hinduism*, compared Thomas Aquinas, the medieval Catholic theologian, with Shankara, whose writings represent the very peak of Hindu thought. It is in this book that Panikkar defined the theme he would develop throughout his later work, the Christ as "the universal symbol of divine-human unity, the human face of God" (Panikkar, 1981).

In the present age of global pluralism, we have multiple encounters between religious traditions. There are now three approaches to theological conversations and studies:

- 1. *Exclusivism.* Exclusivists reaffirm the unique truth of their faith, with minimal if any concessions to the truth claims of others.
- 2. *Pluralism.* Pluralists look on all the traditions as partial but valid perspectives on the ultimate reality. A cautionary note is that pan-tolerance can come upon some moral limits.
- 3. *Inclusivism.* Inclusivists favor dialogue with respect and complete openness but also focus on affirming certain truth claims of their own, possibly the most productive approach to global religious pluralism with provocative insights and the promotion of civic peace between adherents of different traditions.

The Cosmic Christ seems to be a dominant theme of Paul, for example, when he describes the Christ in this way:

He is the image of the invisible God, the
firstborn of all creation; for in him all things
in heaven and on earth were created, things
visible and invisible, whether thrones or
dominions or rulers or powers—all things
have been created through him and for him.
He himself is before all things, and in him
all things hold together. (Colossians 1:15–17)

The term was used by Pierre Teilhard de Chardin
(1881–1955), who said the whole universe, with Christ as
Ruler, is the true fullness of Christianity.

This leads to the premise by Father Richard Rohr
that "from the beginning" means "from the time of the
big bang" fourteen to fifteen billion years ago, the First
Incarnation, when God decided to materialize and to self-
expose. It was through this Cosmic Christ that God "has
made known to us the mystery of his will, according to
his good pleasure that he set forth in Christ" (Ephesians
1:9). Rohr then proposes that two thousand years ago was
the human incarnation of God in Jesus. Rohr emphasizes
that "this earth indeed is the very Body of God, and it is
from this body that we are born, live, suffer, and resurrect
to eternal life" (Rohr, 2010).

Matthew Fox says that this theology is an archetype,

a universal way of seeing the world. It is "the pattern that connects all the atoms and galaxies of the universe; a pattern of divine love and justice that all creatures and all humans bear with them. The Cosmic Christ lives and breathes in Jesus and in all God's children, in all the prophets of religions everywhere, in all creatures of the universe. It is the divine radiance that is present in every galaxy, every porpoise, every blade of grass, and every human" (Fox, 1988).

An ongoing question of mine as a Christian interreligious leader is, "How does the Cosmic Christ relate to other faith traditions?" I feel a strong sense of peace when Buddhist writer, teacher, and scholar Joanna Macy says that the Cosmic Christ is identical with the teachings of the Buddha concerning the interdependence of all creatures. The Buddha nature taps into the Cosmic Christ concept that every soul has a spark of the divine compassion within his or her self, as well.

15

The Postmodern World

I have been confused about being part of the postmodern world. "Have we left the modern world only to go backward?" I would ask.

On occasion I would look around or even drive by Chevrolet showrooms to see if postmodernity was really happening, to see if some of my remembered Chevrolets were once more reappearing. What kinds of Chevrolets were occupying the spaces behind the expansive glass showcases across America's streets?

Was the modern drivers' training car I so enjoyed, the 1959 Chevrolet Impala, with rear wings so large some thought it could easily fly, in there? And sadly, would the 1954 Chevy once more appear, the one that encouraged purchasers to drive it only in the dark of night because it looked and sounded totally like a Fred and Wilma Flintstone car compared to the 1955 Bel Air V-8? I can imagine what it was like driving a 1954 Chevy with these thoughts, because I had three 1954 Fords that, in some similar ways, were put to shame by the '55s.

I have not been the only confused one, for the word postmodern *tends to be misleading. It doesn't bring us back to a bygone era. Instead, it describes major changes in the underlying ways we think, especially in the ways we view truth and reality. The word basically opens discussions about contrasts. It points primarily to the in-between modern era. Before the modern era, the world was considered premodern, an era blindly waiting to drive 1954 Chevys and Fords. Had they only known.*

Life in the postmodern era does make some people nervous about the sky falling, scientifically and theologically. I think the sky is fine; I do like new horizons.

Again, it is not easy to define postmodernism because the word is used in many different areas of study: film, art, literature, architecture, truth, and religion, to name a few. It is easiest to grab by relating postmodernism to modernism.

The 1800s of Western Europe coined the term *modernism* with its being a progressive society. Mechanism, industrialism, literature, and other developments elevated human reason, progress, and authority.

So, postmodernism can be understood as a movement *after* modernism that builds on modernism but often rejects modernism's strict rationalism. Postmodernism is more subjective, believing more in relativism. It considers that truth may be relative, that objective truth may not be knowable.

Modernism can specialize in pursuing truth, absolutism, linear thinking, rationalism, and certainty. Postmodern thinking likely will disagree by saying that this breeds arrogance, inflexibility, and unbalanced control. Postmodernism counters by recognizing that knowledge is shaped by cultures and is controlled by emotions and aesthetics and heritages.

16

Quantum Theory

Human beings progressively build worldviews on scientific, theological, philosophical, and other paths, frequently asking the same questions and exploring the same territories.

For example, since the enlightenment, our universe, with fine-tuned predictability, was considered to be a worldview proof for the existence of the intelligent God. But a new direction surfaced when scientists began to explore the atom, eventually called quantum theory, providing a new adventure for understanding the creation.

Quantum is a Latin word for *amount*. In physics it means the smallest possible discrete unit of any physical property. It has some relationship to the parallel compelling scientific/theological question of the Middle Ages, "How many angels can dance on the head of a pin?" Today's quantum size is purported to be a hundred billion, billion times smaller than the nucleus of an atom.

The earlier organized world of classical physics was shattered by quantum theory and eventually the same dynamic impacted theology. Some people believe that the new physics calls for reevaluation of the traditional understanding of God and reality.

Parallel to systematic (organized) theology, the old physics was given form when scientific thinkers such as Copernicus, Bruno, Kepler, Descartes, and Galileo provided Isaac Newton with adequate resources to explain motion in the universe. With just a few mathematical equations, the *age of reason* was reclassified as the *age of certainty*.

So, with this certainty, with the universe characterized as a huge clock ticking without error, God came to be seen as no longer necessary. In fact, at the beginning of the twentieth century, this view of the universe was held around the clock.

This new physics as we look at it today is actually pretty old, with theoretical and experimental bases established before 1930. The nature and behavior of subatomic particles came to be utterly surprising. It had been thought that the building blocks of the universe were atoms with protons, neutrons, and electrons, a miniature solar system. This is not so about *sub*atomic particles.

As time went on, atomic research led to the Manhattan Project and the atomic bomb; fortunately, quantum physics peacefully brought laser technology and nuclear medicine.

This new perception of reality left the world of mundane prediction and introduced uncertainty and probability. The super-tiny quantum complexities came to bring super-sized question marks about our understanding of the universe with uncertainty being the only certainty. The microuniverse is uncertain, unpredictable, and (for now) impossible to describe.

Some people may desire to return to or remain with the stuff of the good ol' days, when apple pies were pies made with apples instead of almost-endless lists of mysterious ingredients on the sides of the cases holding boxes of the "ready to be baked" frozen pies. Many people who were totally comfortable with the good ol' days feel that whoever came out with suspicious frozen pies had a lot of crust.

But the cases are not closed. Theologians are considering how quantum theory produces a number of theories about reality and God.

Nicholas of Cusa (Germany) was a theologian in the fifteenth century. It's always interesting to note that curiosities of centuries ago encourage us today to be equally curious but with more scientific and theological theories. In his book *The Vision of God*, he talks about the cloud of the impossible.

In spiritual journeys of life, Cusa says that we can consider the contradictions, the cloud of the impossible. For him, and likely for us, the fog filled with contradiction that drifts in is the dilemma that we are finite creatures who have no capacity to grasp the infinite, which is *God*.

Cusa says that the cloud beckons us, sucks us in. We eventually hit a wall. He says that this is good, for we come to realize that the opposites or contradictions in the fog are interwoven, encouraging us to something else, a third way. It's called "the possibility within the impossible" (Nicholas, and Salter, 2007).

Classical physics provided an example. It had been held that nothing happens faster than the speed of light. But in quantum physics, there seem to be instantaneous connections between any two connected particles, no matter how far away they are. It's imaginable, then, to say that nothing is separate from anything.

This has led to what is called *relational theology*, including the idea that all creatures are made in the image of the unknowable. So, the universe that is showing itself in quantum physics is much more connected to theology than was classical physics, which said that the universe is made up of bits of dead, impenetrable matter. Matter now has come to be viewed as something much more mysterious, apparently interconnecting faster than the speed of light, interlinked with the unknown. This scientific exposure relates to the depths of the mysteries of incarnational theology.

Sunday-morning repetitious rituals of education and worship often erase curiosities about the odd and bizarre tenets of the Christian faith. The smell of coffee and cinnamon rolls overwhelms conversations that could be much more investigative.

The contributions of quantum theory, however, potentially can redirect these coffee hour conversations with the parallel odd and bizarre tenets of the new physics. Heuristically speaking, quantum physics and quantum theology possibly can promote space for far-out Sunday-morning topics.

Again, classical physics was a foundation for the age of certainty. Even the nonphysical world (history, psychiatry, theology) was at home with extreme determinism. This is a reason why even today we hear during church coffee hours or classes people saying, "We've always believed this way and always will."

Max Karl Ernst Ludwig Planck (1858–1947) was a German theoretical physicist who originated quantum theory. The theory revolutionized human understanding of atomic and subatomic processes. He was a member of the Lutheran Church in Germany. He was very tolerant toward alternative views and religions.

His quantum hypothesis meant eventually that the determination of classical physics was at an end when Werner Heisenberg came with his "uncertainty principle" in 1926. This meant that particles have not separate, well-defined positions and velocities but a quantum state, a combination of position and velocity. Quantum mechanics predicts not a single definite result but a number of different possible outcomes.

Even the idea of an external world to be objectified, observed, or measured not subject to change had to be abandoned. In fact, the state of the particle or wave came to be seen as determined by the observer. This has led some to believe that human consciousness affects the nature of reality and plays a part in creating reality.

To say it simply, to acknowledge life in an uncertain world means being flexible and adaptable. Everything is true and false to some degree. This view holds that bivalent logic, a classical logic of two values (true and false), doesn't match reality.

This brings us to a world of partial values. This fuzzy logic underlies modes of reasoning that are approximate instead of exact.

When this theory is applied in theological terms, an infinite spectrum of options is opened, broadening the rationality behind our understanding of theology. Fuzzy logic goes beyond a fundamental, relativistic, and dialectic understanding of theology.

In my own experiences of ecumenical and interreligious leadership roles, I can affirm the value of interdisciplinary discussion, intersubjective discussion, and an experiential epistemology, the theory of knowledge that includes the investigation of what distinguishes justified belief from opinion. The irony is that the more information we gather from multiple sources, the clearer and more accurate our picture becomes. However, the more accuracy increases, the more fuzziness creeps into the picture as well.

17

The Observer-Created Universe

A popular view of quantum physicists is that physical objects exist only if and when they are perceived, surprisingly based on experimental data. This view is called the Copenhagen interpretation, which was developed by physicist Niels Bohr.

This stance rejects the existence of an objective world independent from human observation. Pascual Jordan, a theoretical and mathematical physicist who made significant contributions to quantum mechanics and quantum field theory, and other physicists such as Roger Penrose, Martin Rees, Bernard d'Espagnat and David Mermin hold the same creative view.

When Linda and I enjoyed my fiftieth high school class reunion in Montevideo, Minnesota, in 2011, the observed house I grew up in, friends from long ago, and the Salem Lutheran Church building erected in 1950 during my dad's pastorate *reappeared*. However, the water tower across the street from the church was missing. Perhaps our observation did not compel the water tower electrons enough. The old high school appeared to be missing as well, although what appeared to be a bus that took us on a tour was parked on the parking lot next to where the old high school was once observed.

In contrast, one of the tenets of Christianity is committed to realism, the belief that the universe exists apart from observation, because God created the world prior to any human observations for bringing it into existence.

While many physicists support the observer-created universe, many publications present parallels between quantum physics and eastern mysticism. Pantheism describes the unity of all things, evidenced by the organic Eastern mystical view supporting a balanced and fulfilled spiritual life.

The Bible is also referenced with Moses asking, "Who are you?" of the presence felt at the burning bush.

Quantum physics is extremely limited in connecting to the subatomic world; high-speed accelerators for smashing together atomic particles are pretty unusual. With attention on these building blocks of nature to give us a view of reality, the question comes to be, "Does the *sub*atomic world define what is real where these particles come together to form real things in the macrocosm?"

A huge change with quantum theory is that facile models and formulae will no longer explain the nature of the universe. The subatomic world draws us into a new mysterious realm, revealing that our world is more complex than ever imagined. The new physics and quantum theology may bring real fears and astonishment to many.

18

Postmodern Religion

My studies and realizations of the emerging church in Helsinki and Hong Kong definitely validate the above characteristics of quantum theology.

The global postmodern worshiping communities are primarily birthed by people searching for other forms of communal, religious life. There are healthy emphases: sparking curiosity, stirring imagination, and opening reflections on what it is to be religious in light of what is actually taking place.

Any religion that is influenced by postmodernism and postmodern philosophies is called postmodern religion. There is not an attempt to get rid of religion; quite the opposite. It is a philosophical approach to religion that carefully considers orthodox or established assumptions. Postmodern religion views realities as plural and subjective and dependent on an individual's worldview.

Postmodern philosophy professes that society constantly changes. This strengthens the perspective of the individual but discounts the strength of institutions, well documented by dwindling attendances in mainline Christian denominations.

Double-belonging is one example of this as individuals seek to draw eclectically on diverse religious beliefs, practices, and rituals, incorporating the diversity into their worldviews.

Societal groups who face discrimination, marginalization, or disenfranchisement are sometimes drawn to postmodern religious thinking given the opportunity to connect with a version of reality or truth that does not exclude them.

I personally have not chosen to be an isolated Lutheran. I value a host of friends of diverse traditions. I have never regretted this. On the contrary, when I am occasionally distanced from ecumenical and interreligious interchanges I become a little listless. I do believe that a dilemma of many mainline congregations today comes from an ignorance or a lack of openness to new, and in ways, better traditions.

One of my favorite places on earth is the *Abbey of Gethsemani*, Trappist, Kentucky. This is because the air is filled with the life and rule of St. Benedict, and it's contagious. The first words you see as you enter are "Let

All Guests That Come Be Received Like Christ" (C.53, St. Benedict).

Benedict was gifted to find a practical way to bring the order and stability of the gospel into the chaos and insecurity of life. It was realized that this does not automatically happen in daily life unless first the people who implement it are converted spiritually. It is said that the spirituality of St. Benedict (with a footnote that it was not "his" but Christ's) had "to root up and tear down, to destroy and demolish" the residue of original sin, in order "to build and to plant" the reign of God.

Therefore, what is it to be religious in today's world, especially as we reflect on a changing era and different ways of being human?

Vibrant communities, I believe, can be those who are open to transformation by reaching out with eyes open to the world.

Without question, communities of mainline traditions are being impacted both positively and negatively by changes in global cultural patterns and world economies. I believe that the future of the religious traditions can be bright when we are open to necessary adaptations; the future of the traditions can become bleak if we isolate ourselves and try to maintain strategies that have been in place for long periods of time but no longer work. Survivability of communities can be realized with appropriate change, which also brings a renewed sense of identity, focus, and fun.

Not everyone thinks this way. Isolation is comfortable for some. But doing that which has been done for decades causes communities to think that they have the truth, the whole truth, and nothing but the truth. With this kind of thinking, communities easily come to bask in their own traditions even when they are pushing people away.

In my Lutheran tradition, it is hard for many people to change, to break out of established patterns and (sometimes empty) rituals. This phenomenon is at the heart of cooling hearts, disunity, and declining participation. As an ecumenical and interreligious leader, I can also say it is often frustrating to observe enthusiasm for new relationships on local, national, and global levels and then eventually realize only occasional and isolated celebrations.

But it's a great daily habit, even if it's metaphorical, to wash out our ears, to clean our glasses, to blow our noses, to comb our hair, to trim our mustaches, and to dive into some deep cleansing waters. That last one is a bit scary for me, but many of you are good swimmers.

In the January 2007 issue of *The Lutheran* magazine,

Presiding Bishop Mark Hanson of the Evangelical Lutheran Church in America stated in an article, "Tackling Membership Decline," that the ELCA had lost two hundred seventy-five thousand members in the last five years. He also spoke of the biggest hurdle standing in the way of membership growth: the fear of change.

Without the fear of change, I was privileged to study the Global Emerging Church Movement on a sabbatical in 2008. The application for this sabbatical followed my reading an article about *The Finnish Experiment: Liturgical Evangelism,* by Pastor F. Dean Lueking in *The Christian Century* magazine, June 13, 2006. I was confident that the dynamics realized in Finland (and Hong Kong as well) could provide the setting of spiritual and evangelical renewal called for by Presiding Bishop Mark Hanson.

At the heart of this Finnish experiment (and in Hong Kong) is a common thread that holds a variety of Christian traditions and world religions together. In the lingo of the Global Emerging Church, this thread is called nondualistic thinking.

19

Postmodern Religion and Nondualistic Thinking

Nondualistic thinking is contrasted with a more familiar mind-set, dualistic thinking, which holds positions as black or white, right or wrong. Dualistic thinking can put a person, a tradition, or even a congregation on a pedestal with the dismissal of those who differ.

Even the concepts of radical openness and nondualistic thinking have shaped my thinking without awareness of their definitions. For about forty-five years now I have personally found my desire to be open to diverse people and ideas enhanced by not mirroring a stereotypical Lutheran pastor.

My success has been very good, for it has been common for people to say, "Jepson, you don't seem very religious, even when you're decked out in your black suit, black socks, black shoes, black shoelaces, black belt, black wallet, and black clerical shirt with a white Roman collar."

I respond with, "Thanks!"

My transition from being a conservative, pietistic, dualistic Lutheran Swede began in seminary in 1966. I decided to expand and test my improvisational personality. Sure enough, this not only impacted my lifestyle but enhanced my self-worth and brought new adventures and relationships.

My more daring personality and coseminarian Mickey Dobbins's amazingly parallel personality brought us a lot of the time to Mama Rosa's, a great watering hole in Dinky Town near the University of Minnesota in Minneapolis. We liked the music, the pizza, the cute servers, the beer, and conversations with the people around us.

One step up in the SW corner of this establishment was a little area with a table and chairs usually inhabited by guys from the gay community.

When Dobbins and I weren't at Mama Rosa's, we spent a lot of time checking out other opportunities for meeting girls, specifically student nurses at Lutheran hospitals. Just prior to my loving beer, I was fortunate to hear a car approaching the seminary with a flat tire. A very attractive girl was driving the car. I agreed to change her tire with the stipulation that she go on a date with me. She agreed and introduced me to my very first beer on that date, Miller High Life.

With these busy social schedules, Dobbins and I often studied for classes late into the nights.

The 1960s had some rigid suspicions about those *different* people one step up. But for some reason, Dobbins and I dared to believe that they were on the same level with all human beings ... girls, atheists, monks, professors, street people, the cute barmaids at Mama Rosa's, and even Norwegian Lutherans.

The proposal for my pastoral psychology project was rapidly approaching. What to do? No problem. What better experience could there be than to explore a meeting of the minds from the heterosexual and homosexual communities?

My proposal was approved, the "Convocation on Homosexuality" at Northwestern Lutheran Theological Seminary. What a great day it was, for the human beings we knew from the SW corner, one step up, were the principal presenters.

A year of internship occurs in seminary during the third year. My request for that year included a desire to be placed in a location quite different from Minnesota, where

I could experience diversity, where one could not find a Lutheran behind every tree.

My requests were fulfilled. I would develop a new leisure/recreation model ministry in Island Park, Idaho, for three months, on the west side of Yellowstone National Park, sponsored by six Christian denominations and the Board of American Missions of the Lutheran Church in America. The model gathered information for proposing religious strategies in a society that was becoming more centered on leisure and recreation. During the next nine months, my internship would continue at First Lutheran Church, Idaho Falls, Idaho.

Idaho Falls at that time had the largest percentage population of Mormons in the United States. My studies of the Church of Jesus Christ of Latter Day Saints were magnified with friendships from that tradition. The membership of First Lutheran provided unusual resources with an abundance of individuals employed at the Atomic Energy Commission.

Again, these new adventures were preceded with another heuristic journey, an intentional journey that leaves the world of divisive narrow-mindedness toward a goal that is not clear.

This preparatory journey provided new horizon-thinking

on interstate highways. Dobbins's internship was going to be in Bethlehem, Pennsylvania. He decided to visit his family first in Billings, Montana, conveniently on my route to Idaho. We decided to drive our vehicles to Billings and visit with his family.

My 1963 Ford Falcon two-door hardtop ran with great anticipation. Dobbins's 1955 2-door Bel Air Chevy presented a very enviable contrast.

Our radios blared with the music of the North Dakota tourist jingle, "North to Dakota!" with the voice-over telling us to "hop on Interstate 94." That we did.

What a nice welcome it was in Billings. Dobbins's mom opened the door and gave me a big kiss. My injury was minor. She forgot that she had a toothpick between her lips.

One evening in Billings we went to Grandma's Pub. We left through a back door and ran down a dark alley from two rowdy guys who didn't care for us. Just previous to this encounter, I had talked with some of the band members.

Several days later, I settled into my A-frame cabin in Island Park. It had become easier to find, for the youths of First Lutheran had put together a little sculpture that they nailed on a tree composed of a halo and angel's wings.

A nice pub (Doc's) in nearby West Yellowstone, Montana, came to be a favorite place for gatherings with new friends. Wouldn't you know … the band I knew, for they had recently played at Grandma's! With our continuing conversations, they often invited me, the park chaplain, to have breakfast with them.

Radical openness. Nondualistic thinking.

In Island Park I visited 3,303 campsites during June, July, and August, 1968. No hidden agendas. No proselytizing. Open to diverse treasures shared by thousands of people in an appropriate, subtle context called *trust.*

20

More Nondualistic Connections

From 1976 to 1993 and 1998 to 2001, on both sides of the Ohio River with few Lutherans, my identity as a mission developer was wonderfully out of focus, a great advantage for open conversations. Often people would say, "So what is a Lutherian?" In 2008, my nondualistic thinking patterns were expanded again in Helsinki and Hong Kong.

The *Thomas Mass* in Helsinki was named after the doubting Thomas, another person who early on considered leaving the faith tradition. This mass began as a response to the phenomenon of dwindling church attendances in Finland, about twenty years before this occurred in Canada and the United States.

Two fractured communities lived side by side in Helsinki, the "believers" and the "doubters." About 2 to 3 percent of the 85 percent Lutheran population of the city participated in the life of the traditional church.

With a commitment to an ecumenical process, people attracted a melting of theologies and placed them into the classical structures of the mass. This common ground of trust brought reality to the question, "Are we honest doubters or dishonest believers? Where do we stand together?" They brought traditions with a severe openness to each other.

In an earlier, parallel way, the Tao Fong Shan Christian Centre (Linda's and my home away from home) in Hong Kong had its beginnings with Karl Ludvig Reichelt, a missionary to China sent in 1903 by the Norwegian Lutheran Missionary Society. Reichelt visited the great monastery of Wei Shan, which left a positive impression, motivating him to study Chinese religions and philosophies, including Buddhism.

At his invitation, Buddhist monks who traveled between monasteries would come to study with Christians the Buddhist resources as well as Christian scriptures at Tao Fong Shan. In fact, the architecture of the Christian Centre replicates that of the Buddhist monasteries. These monks came because they were recognized and affirmed instead of being labeled as "those of the wrong tradition."

My mentors in Hong Kong were Pastors John LeMond and Ted Zimmerman.

Back to Finland.

Over seven hundred people were welcomed at the first Thomas Mass in Helsinki's Mikael Agricola Lutheran Church in 1988, and the popularity of the mass has not declined. Nondualistic features behind the mass exist in an association of people by crossing parochial boundaries.

Nondualistic thinking is evident as the mass does not have a clear, developed theological line; instead, it reaches out alongside the Lutheran tradition as a mission to those who otherwise might be alienated by avoiding the idea of two classes, the "saved ones" and "the rest." The openness of the Lord's Table to everyone, without exception, baptized or not, is a hallmark.

The Thomas Mass came into being when a group of priests, active parishioners, and academics were gathered to consider how the liturgy of the Lutheran Church could be brought closer to people who had become alienated from the church. This group included high church people, the charismatic tradition, people influenced by Taize, liberals, evangelicals, and a postmodern influence. In Helsinki, the mass engages a group of fifty to seventy laity in a variety of tasks each week. It has spread over Finland and to dozens of locations in Sweden, Norway, Denmark, and Germany.

Helsinki's urban culture, the secular culture that has come to define the people's needs, points to the foundations for the Thomas Mass. It reflects many of the characteristics that dominate the urban American culture today.

The culture in the United States parallels Europe in experiencing a dwindling participation in the life of the church. The Thomas Mass in Finland assumes that many of those who stayed away from the church did so because of patterns of disunity, exclusiveness, and boring liturgies.

Pastor F. Dean Lueking, in his *The Christian Century* article (June 13, 2006), wrote this:

> "THE TROUBLE with the church in Finland," a Finnish Lutheran pastor told me, "is that everybody loves it and nobody goes there." Some 85 percent of the 5.2 million Finns are disengaged from the church except for brief pit stops for baptism, confirmation, marriage and burial.

Lueking then goes on to explain how Olli Valtonen and Miikka Ruokanen introduced a mass for people disenchanted with or alienated from the church.

Lueking does emphasize that the United States is still untried territory, perhaps because US evangelism today is prevalently person-centered rather than liturgically based.

In the United States, many people feel disconnected for the same reasons as was the case in Helsinki; however, an additional "bad taste" of the church in America comes from principles of consumerism with brand names such as Lutheran, Presbyterian, United Church of Christ, United Methodist, Episcopal and so forth, which loudly proclaim dualistic thinking and disunity.

The Thomas Mass focuses on the Eucharist, the activity of God that draws people together. In Finland, this sacramental emphasis centers on its severe openness to the diversities of God's people, providing an environment of contemplation and listening in the presence of God instead of rigidity and isolation.

21

Rigidity and Isolation

I believe a pattern of frozen rigidity, dualistic thinking, is strong in American culture/religious traditions. Openness to diversity is often narrow, and therefore commitment to one's own perception of politics and God can become very entrenched. This dualistic thinking may have little or no grounding in scripture or history and can lead to "folk religion." Folk religion, sometimes termed as popular belief, consists of ethnic or regional concepts under the umbrella of a religion. Unfortunately, this pious and sometimes naïve "certain beyond a doubt" belief, which may remain quite primitive, can be passed on from generation to generation.

One of my favorite dreams in seminary was to eventually project progressive theology into congregational life. After all, from my front seat in every classroom and lecture hall

I imagined how I might thaw out frigid rigidities that were not willing to open some windows as spring arrives.

Thirty degrees below zero, however, becomes strangely something to be proud about. I do feel that the less common frigid temperatures of Mishawaka compared to Minnesota's records are nostalgic and have kind of a warm and good feeling. You see, Lutherans such as I who grew up "up there" in Minnesota are proudly and somewhat biblically called "the frozen chosen people of God."

When lake effect snow tries to mimic horizontal Minnesota blizzards, it is so reminiscent of the Lutheran homeland that Linda has caught me a couple of times returning to my Swedish dialect of years past. This was corrected for the most part when we became Hoosiers as we left thirty degrees below zero to drive up to our new home in New Albany, Indiana, on December 31, 1975, at approximately 10:37 p.m. with a temperature of sixty degrees *above* zero.

These nostalgic frigid rigidity memories that come from plummeting temperatures admittedly make the mysteries of spring very attractive. Warming temperatures bring guarded excitement as one starts to enjoy new, almost forgotten experiences of northern life, being freed of the confinements of three pairs of socks and insulated boots, of scarves and gloves and parkas, of frozen locks on car doors, of dead batteries and frozen pipes, and yeah, even the fear of being pierced by a six-foot icicle, or worse yet, by a seven-footer. Frigid rigidity, I guess, prepares one for that breath of fresh air that comes as one carefully opens a window in the kitchen or relaxes with the freedom to park on either side of the streets with rivulets being fed from melting snow banks without worrying about which side of the street is to be plowed.

However, for some, the cold winds of winter seem to remain. The windows are left closed, and the air-conditioners are turned on.

What is the typical frigid rigidity of life in communities? It happens when there is too much climate control when the need is to be invigorated with an early spring. Traditions require refocusing to continue and expand connections between people who are changing in contemporary generational and pluralistic cultures.

Institutional religion, like other institutions, is experiencing a broad process of sociological change and transformation. This process, called world-historical change, is not new but instead repetitive in eras of human history.

Because of these massive cultural shifts, many

communities freeze. One of the reasons for this is linked to institutions that have outdated bases for building relationships.

Don't get me wrong. Patterns for relationship building of many years ago were great. My first years as a parish pastor included my attending many women's circle Bible studies. They were a great draw in Douglas County, Minnesota.

Along with the Bible studies, coffee and coffee cakes, and small sandwiches, and cookies and "barsss" (Swedish dialect applied to "bars") were highlights. I always noticed that the women were also very health conscious. When the barsss were passed around a second time, a common response was, "They're so big! Donna, would you like to share half of this one with me?" I really enjoyed this, and contained my laughter, for each of the "whole" barsss measured six-eighths by six-eighths by six-eighths of an inch.

These times were great and warm, but socially they won't be a strong draw some forty-five years later. I do know, fortunately, that these congregations have indeed opened the windows for change and continue to thrive. However, many religious communities find themselves today to be essentially the last institutions to be no longer relational. Instead, Apple stores or Starbucks are among the new communal places for building ongoing relationships.

Places are moving around with technological developments. Online shopping and fewer brick-and-mortar buildings now transfer people to become texters while driving from being people who sat safely in back pews admiring stained glass windows or Gothic architecture.

This world-historical change *can* introduce new resources that can successfully provide formats for relationship building. An opportune time was during the national catastrophe on September 11, 2001. Americans wanted to participate in various communities with chat rooms, intimacy, and sharing. The people did come that first weekend, but they did not return because they were generally met with the rational, the logical, and preaching.

M. Rex Miller, theologian, futurist, and communicator, says that in this digital culture a negative shift is taking place in mega-churches as well, for their great programs are becoming businesslike with a dwindling sense of community.

World-historical changes occur in eras of human history. Such was the case with the following four periods of church history in terms of dominant communication styles.

- **The Oral Culture:** The church was tightly knit; the clergy were symbolic hierarchy. There was not linear learning with books and creeds. Instead, insight was based on liturgical or ritualistic patterns.

- **The Print Culture:** Reformation until 1950. In the oral culture, the "message" and the "messenger" were one and the same. With the Gutenberg printing press came linear thought, with the message separated from the messenger. Individuals could evaluate on their own.

- **The Broadcast Era:** With the advent of television, people no longer needed training or background to absorb the message. Catechisms became boring prescriptions. The continual stimulation of television brought very little content, leading to *celebration* churches.

- **The Digital Culture:** In contrast to the Broadcast Era model, this culture is interactive and raw; the content is built with what the audience brings. This is a reason why, prior to the digital culture, people didn't talk constantly on pay phones on street corners.

The current complex changes of societies can be overwhelming. On the other hand, changes can encourage us to open new doors leading to exciting adventures. Adventures are bold, usually risky, and have uncertain outcomes. Adventurous experiences create within people psychological and physiological arousal or enthusiasm. Bear in mind, they *can* bring negative enthusiasm (frigid fear), but they can also bring positive, "thaw"tful relationships.

Communities with frigid fear can lock out people who have an overwhelming spiritual curiosity and are not able to find communities of faith that provide more mystery and more openness. This explains the growing popularity in America of options: Eastern religions, Native American rituals, Wicca, and new age movements.

Roman Catholic Father Richard Rohr participated in the Thomas Mass in Helsinki on June 8, 2008. His severe openness with the Lutherans is envisioned often in what he says. For example, "Life is about discovering the right questions more than having the right answers." Or, "We do not think ourselves into a new way of living, but we live ourselves into a new way of thinking."

22

Introducing and Sustaining Postmodern Religion in America

One's commitment/noncommitment to a religion can be tied to secular cultures. I am not saying that religious traditions necessarily become culture-driven, but instead that religions are tuned differently by what the secular culture allows or appreciates.

The American culture is very noisy, where talking is more important than listening. This is why it takes patience in bringing what has become comfortable in other parts of the world to America. Because there are large learning curves as we bring this emerging movement to America, there must be intentional respect for the learners and the entire community.

First English Lutheran Church of Mishawaka, Indiana, came to be a model lab.

After my retirement as pastor of First English, I became the associate director of the United Religious Community of St. Joseph County, Indiana, where ecumenical and interreligious ideas included many of the same patterns.

The Emerging Church Movement could be very frightening for a congregation such as First English and therefore had to be introduced with kind sensitivity. This is very interesting, because the Emerging Church Movement parallels many emerging movements, including economics, businesses, energy resources, health care, and technologies.

Emerging movements surface when some parts of systems work and others don't. With appropriate evaluation and/or change, new systems can emerge. Without evaluation and/or change, systems can become submerged.

The Emerging Church is still becoming; it is not antitraditions but parallel traditions, sometimes called the hyphenated church or traditions emergence. Europe and Scandinavia have experienced this movement for quite some time. When the emerging church came to be experienced at First English, this congregation joined a minute minority, especially in the Evangelical Lutheran Church in America.

A primary premise of the emerging church is to recognize that all institutions, including the church, eventually become too preoccupied with divisive self-preservation, divisive self-maintenance, and divisive self-perpetuation (i.e., we are right, and they are not right).

The Emerging Church Movement is called global because it is very wide, happening within the Lutheran, Roman Catholic, Anglican, Pentecostal, and other traditions.

The Global Emerging Church Movement can be identified with four categories:

- An honest, broad, consensus-building, and ecumenical Jesus scholarship instead of exclusive scholarship. Interreligious scholarship can also be appropriate.
- A contemplative, pondering mind that is open to the Holy Spirit and this *wider* scholarship.
- Considers the possibilities that what was thought to be nonnegotiable can be.
- Carefully, and most slowly, develops structures that actually proclaim the church instead of simply establishing another tradition.

One of the reasons for enthusiasm hinges on the fact

that the Global Emerging Church Movement runs parallel to many postmodern, postlinear, and postenlightenment reformations. Larry L. Rasmussen squarely provides a holistic vision for this in which society and nature are understood as a single interrelated community. He calls the present world environment the *shock of recognition* that lead to conversions. He says that humanity is called to reexamine everything. This calls religion, ethics, and environmental science to a single vision for creating a sustainable community of the planet (Rasmussen, 1996).

These ideas and sustainable involvements of parishioners and the ecumenical and interreligious communities were embraced in many ways in northern Indiana.

- At First English, the introduction was nondualistic, with the creation of two optional ways to worship and learn, called *parallel tracks*. Parallel tracks came to be seen as a great and sensitive way to experience postmodernism without conflict.
  - *The first track* of worship and education was for those who continued to feel comfortable with the ways things always have been done.
  - *The second track* of worship and education was built on ecumenical/interreligious contemplative/ meditative prayer. The environmental space

in the deep chancel was altered physically to accommodate more flexibility for meditation and also yoga. The exterior prayer garden also reflected the same surroundings. Ecumenical and interreligious education drew participants from many diverse traditions.

○ *The second track for confirmands* (seventh through ninth grades) in this postlinear/postmodern age had no line-after-line faith statements that can easily become farewell addresses for leaving faith traditions.

■ Confirmation Sunday in practice has changed remarkably not only in my lifetime but also during my years of ordained ministry. This change is not unusual in the Lutheran tradition, for our unique heritage is to be the reforming movement with the church catholic.

Martin Luther reformed confirmation from a sacrament to a rite. He had no desire to continue the practice of *Chrismation*, a supplementary outpouring of the Holy Spirit beyond the sacrament of holy baptism. He said that confirmation as a sacrament would be fine if it would be kept a secret from God. As a rite, it simply is a good, formal process of evaluation.

Young people are experiencing a changing religious landscape. It's good that the Lutheran tradition and many others are open to change, for when a tradition fails to connect with its audience, it begins to die.

The first hundred years of the church saw Christians as people who liked lively spoken versus written recollections of Jesus's impact on the world, known as the oral tradition. But eventually there came to be a heavy, boring "page-after-page" set of doctrines pounded with reluctant response into young people instead of conversational enjoyment.

For many years my wife, Linda, and I taught young people by not spoon-feeding mesmerizing memorization but instead by providing four or five learning styles so diverse students could be highly engaged for at least a quarter or one-fifth of the time instead of being put to sleep. I wrote concise thematic statements, and Linda illustrated them in comic page form. The characters were quite hilarious.

Today, young people no longer carry heavy briefcases filled with books on doctrine as I once did. As time went on some of my books yellowed and fell apart.

- At the United Religious Community, we focused on gatherings.
  - ◦ *The Cellar,* a coffeehouse in the basement, was established for interreligious presentations and conversations for educators and college and university students. Some students were given class extra credit by their institutions.
  - ◦ The annual countywide *Tastes of Thanksgiving* featured foods from many ethnic and religious heritages. Each year traditions provided presentations such as dancing by the youths from the Sikh community. The prayers and conversations reflected the reality that these events celebrated the entire cosmos.

23

Worship and the Cloud of the Impossible

Quantum theory in chapter 16 was reviewed as a new perception of reality that left prediction and introduced uncertainty and probability. Quantum physics and the super-tiny quantum complexities are, for now, impossible to describe. In turn, theologians considered how quantum theory brings a number of theories about reality and God.

In chapter 16 it was noted that the fifteenth-century theologian Nicholas of Cusa said that in spiritual journeys of life, people can consider contradictions, the fog that accompanies the dilemma that we, as finite creatures, have no capacity to grasp the infinite, which is God.

This notion by Cusa to consider this fog continues to be paramount for our thinking today. As we enter the cloud, we hit a wall. He said that this is good as we begin to realize that the opposites or contradictions in the fog are interwoven.

This leads us to a third way, called "the possibility within the impossible."

Recall that this introduces what is called relational theology with the concept that all creatures are made in the image of the unknowable. Matter comes to be viewed as something much more mysterious, interlinked with the unknown, comparable to the depths of the mysteries of incarnational theology.

What we call matter becomes myth, something subtle, interconnecting everything faster than the speed of light with the unknown. Without this more sophisticated discourse, we will simply be satisfied with a wide range of philosophical, spiritual, and poetical metaphors.

We often blindly continue with old perceptions of reality. Theologians continue to work with a geocentric universe in mind as they talk about church. A geocentric theory is an astronomical theory that describes the universe as a geocentric system (i.e., a system that puts the planet earth in the center of the universe and describes other objects from the point of view of this speck in the cosmos).

To put theology in a different context for church, it is to be remembered (or accepted) that we live in a galaxy-filled space that began some 13.8 billion years ago with the big bang. About 10 billion years later biological life on earth began. Human beings emerged about two hundred thousand years ago as latecomers.

Neil deGrasse Tyson, astrophysicist and science communicator, portrays the brevity of human existence. He prorates 13.8 billion years with an imaginary twelve-month calendar. This "cosmic calendar" shows human history takes place in the last minute, of the last hour, of the last day of the universe. This cosmic picture is a reminder of the vastness and complexity of God's creation and our minuscule role.

The parallel tracks at First English ignited the warm fires of sophisticated discourse. Parishioners not only participated but also generated creative analyses and foundational materials in the contributions that follow. The congregation's openness was captured with this slogan: "Where Improvisation Is Built on Tradition."

- **Richard Allen: Consider a distinction between belief and trust.**

Belief concerns what I think I know. Like all people, I believe a great many things, in the sense of accepting that the contents of such beliefs are true.

Trust concerns my affiliations, my ties to other people and to the world. Thus, I believe that rising concentrations of carbon dioxide in the atmosphere will lead to profound changes in climate. I accept this as true because I trust those engaged in the scientific endeavor. Though not a scientist myself, I feel an affiliation with the people who are.

I teach a course at Indiana University South Bend called "Religions of the West." At the start, I say that the course will deal with Judaism, Christianity, and Islam. I then add that there is a fourth option, which we also need to consider: none of the above. In the Americas, Europe, and the Middle East, many people have little or no affiliation with, or engagement in, any form of religious practice. In Britain and France, on a Sunday morning, about 5 percent of the population attend services in Christian churches.

Pastor Len Jepson's sabbatical gave him the opportunity to deepen his engagement with the emerging church in Europe and Asia—and to bring the fruits of this engagement back to our parish, First English Lutheran Church. The key to the idea of the emerging church, as I understand it, is its emphasis on affiliation, on trust. In the emerging church, people are invited to become engaged—crucially, to partake of the sacraments—straight away. Affiliation is not dependent, either formally or implicitly, on a person's subscribing to a given set of beliefs.

One major advantage to this approach is that it avoids an antagonistic relationship with postmodernity, particularly with science. It is common for evangelical protestants to distrust, and reject, the practices and conclusions of today's scientists: they do not believe in the reality of evolution, climate change, or the earth sciences. Instead, they believe in static species, a climate that human activity does not affect, and an earth far younger than the generally accepted number of 4.5 billion years. I think this is a dead end. Such an antagonistic relationship commits people to believing ideas that cannot be sustained. It also commits them to disaffiliation from the practices and practitioners of science, to systemic distrust.

The emerging church, by contrast, has no quarrel with scientific postmodernity. And crucially, it sees engaging in such a quarrel—in setting up a conflict over beliefs—as both beside the point and an impediment to engagement in a religious life.

To put this positively: The Christian life is fundamentally a matter of trust. Luther understood this well, as did, long before him, St. Augustine of Hippo. In this sense, the emerging church is very traditional. It seeks to adapt and reinvigorate the context for living a religious life in our postmodern world and increasingly secular age. It seeks, in other words, to create a place, a community, a church to which they can belong, and within which their own ways of living a religious life can flourish. And it seeks to do so in a way that recognizes that living in Augustine's two cities—the city of God and the human city—is an inescapable reality of life.

But why trust? Why be Christian (or Jewish or Muslim, or Buddhist) at all? Why not just stay home? Why not think that the human city is all there is?

At First English Lutheran, the sign along the road carries the message, "*A Contemplative Parish.*" Contemplation involves silence, waiting, listening. It seeks to quiet the internal monologue of beliefs, evaluations, and editorials for the sake of something other, for another sound or voice can only be attended to when the monologue stops. The practice of such contemplation, either during regular Sunday-morning services or during the "pearls of God" on Sunday evenings, can appear to a person both as an invitation and as a challenge. The challenge, of course, is to be quiet. And the invitation? Luther famously wrote that "faith is a work of God in us."

The sign extends an invitation to those driving along the road. The practice of contemplation extends another. Fundamentally, the reality of the "emerging church"— indeed, of a community that is always in the process of emerging—lies in people's trust that this latter invitation receives its answer.

- **Eric Petersen. A focus of the sabbatical was on the _relevance_ of the church to portions of people in today's world.**

I agree with Pastor Jepson in how we as a society are in the post-Christian era. It wasn't that long ago when people, confronted with the fact that they "didn't go to church," would usually _claim_ membership in a faith and even a particular congregation. In contrast, today people who are not active in a faith are no longer defensive but instead ask, "Why should I be?"

In my experience, most people acknowledge the importance of a spiritual component in their lives but do not feel that the church can deliver.

There is a theory in marketing that no product ever completely disappears, even when it doesn't deliver. This is true of the institutional church as it is _traditionally_ known. A portion of the 23 percent of the population that still attends worship is not focused on what is lacking spiritually; instead, they want their pastors to do a better job at getting and keeping members and improving finances.

I reasoned (many years ago) that if I became a good

church member, I could overcome my problems with spiritual formation.

In my case, and in similar cases, the conventional church cannot solve these problems. I believe the church *has* the answers for solving the spiritual dilemmas of people ... but often doesn't reach out to those who *need* help, unlike the ministry of Jesus and his followers.

This is where I believe the sabbatical can fit in. Our study of nondualistic thinking makes it possible to consider that *anyone* can be a member of the faith.

The Thomas Mass in Helsinki looks very much like a service typical of the confessional faiths of Christianity, with one exception. To participate completely in the service does not require one to be baptized first. To me, the most significant sacrament of the church is Holy Communion, because it gives a sense of belonging.

On Sunday nights we have an ongoing dialogue of the emerging church, discussion of nondualistic thinking, guided meditation, and contemplative prayer. As a regular attendee at the *pearls of God,* I have yet to go home without a level of rejuvenation.

While I believe this is a process that can work, the question is, "Will it work, really?" Will it result in greater involvement of this congregation? Will it attract new members? No one can answer these questions, but I still believe that every society needs some form of spiritual structure.

As for me, I am grateful that Pastor Jepson was able to participate in the sabbatical and that we have the opportunity to be on the cutting edge of spiritual growth.

- **Kathryn Coleman**

Since Pastor Len Jepson returned from his sabbatical, First English Lutheran Church is gently experiencing new ideas and new ways of worship. First and foremost is the introduction (or perhaps reintroduction) of the importance of silence in worship. We now consider and call ourselves a *contemplative* congregation.

Many of Pastor's sermons include scriptures and lessons that illustrate the importance of contemplation, that we must listen to hear God, and that silence is the only way to truly achieve that. We have begun to practice fifteen minutes of silence before each Sunday-morning service as a way to prepare our hearts for worship.

In addition to the small steps we are taking during our traditional Sunday-morning worship, Pastor has opened the church on Sunday evenings with a new worship called *pearls of God*. This time together is spent totally in prayer as we use worship beads to guide us through an hour of contemplation.

I have found that the calming effect of this time in the church, with the lights very low and candles lit, is a wonderful way to prepare for the week to come. This time of silence and prayer is another step toward offering the emerging church as an inviting and alternative way of worship for church members as well as the South Bend/Mishawaka community.

- **Jean Whetstone**

I have been very fascinated with the changes that have been taking place in the emerging church. I have been participating in a discussion group for nondualistic thinking and have enjoyed learning and participating in the engaging conversations that have taken place.

I made my confirmation when I was eleven years old, and the only thing I remember is all the memorizing we had to do for all the creeds and the Lord's Prayer. Pastor Jepson has been leading information sessions on what it is to be a Lutheran, and I am getting more from those sessions than from my confirmation at my young age.

Maybe that isn't what confirmation was supposed to be about, but I think learning about our doctrine should have been. I have become more involved in my church since Pastor Jepson has led our congregation than I have for some time. I feel more fulfilled spiritually than I have my whole adult life. It has helped me to be more open in my thinking and less judgmental.

- **Mark and Aurora Nieding**

The emerging church is an exciting new initiative we are undertaking here at First English Lutheran, which we believe will help breathe not only new life into our congregation but also serve as a means of growing our spirituality by challenging us to view and think about the body of Christ in different ways.

After returning from sabbatical, Pastor Len conducted the morning Eucharist service of the Tao Fong Shan Christian Centre of Hong Kong as a means of introducing the emerging church to First English. The service included extended periods of silence for contemplative prayer and also featured offerings of flowers, incense, and water symbolizing constant renewal, the prayers of humanity, and our baptism.

Within a few weeks of returning, Pastor Len introduced contemplative prayer sessions on Sunday nights—guided meditation using the *pearls of God*. At first, Aurora and I weren't too sure what to think about that. While the Tao Fong Shan service was a change of pace, this sounded like some new age exercise, a retro-sixties thing for retired flower children. Although neither of us had much experience with meditation, guided or otherwise, we decided to give it a try, reasoning that if we didn't like it, we wouldn't have to go back.

After we arrived at church that night, Pastor explained the concept of using beads as a focusing tool for both meditation and prayer, a tradition that went back to the earliest Christian times but that had fallen out of favor over the past few centuries. It was, he told us, an *ancient future* movement, a means of rediscovering our Christian roots.

Pastor then handed us each a set of pearls—beads of various sizes and colors, each of which represents a different aspect of the faith—and took us through the pearls one at a time, introducing the concept behind each one: The God Pearl. The "I" Pearl. The "Pearl of Desert." In between each pearl, we had a lengthy silence, during which we sat and breathed and concentrated on listening—listening to the silence.

The experience was invigorating! Both Aurora and I were quite tired when we arrived that night, having spent most of the weekend running errands and working in our yard and flower garden. Above all, we were concerned about not being able to give this new experience our full attention.

Both of us felt refreshed when we left. It was like we had tapped into some new energy source, a wellspring of spirituality that replenished us. We knew right then Pastor was onto something.

We went home that night marveling at how rejuvenated we both felt, particularly Aurora, who used to get the "Sunday Night Blues"—feeling down and depressed that the weekend was over and dreading the prospect of having to face Monday morning—really bad. Since then, we have regularly attended "pearls," and Aurora no longer gets the Sunday night blues. Instead, she draws strength from pearls, from the contemplative prayer we experience there, and it helps her to welcome transitioning to another workweek.

For us, the most appealing part of the emerging church—as experienced through contemplative prayer— is the silence.

Many people these days don't understand silence. When confronted with it, they don't know how to react or what to do. The reason why is all the noise we experience in our lives—the constant bombardment of sounds and images from television, computers, cell phones, text messages, the radio, movies. It starts the minute you wake up and doesn't stop until the second you turn off the lights at night and go to sleep. It's continuous stimulation all day long, and not just when we're around other people at our workplace or the store or in a restaurant—it happens when we're alone, too, driving our cars or at home. We have to have something, some kind of sound in the form of a human voice talking to us or music, to dispel the silence because we can't handle it.

The emerging church understands the value of silence, because it knows the quiet time, the time when we force ourselves to settle down and our minds to be still, the time when God speaks to us; all we have to do is listen.

Pastor Len has actively incorporated more silence into the traditional Sunday service as well—from more quiet time for contemplation prior to the service to lengthened pauses during the service—encouraging congregants to sit and listen to the still, small voice.

A crucial aspect of the emerging church is the premise that doubting is allowed; it's okay to not know definitely that God exists. For us, this has truly been liberating in that we no longer felt an obligation to "figure it out"— to try to logically prove that, yes, the divine is real, and by the way, here's his address and cell phone number. By subtracting the requirement for proof, it leaves us free to simply trust. Trusting in the unknown, experiencing the freedom in not having to know, is faith defined.

Pastor Len has spoken about this numerous times as part of his sermons as well as at "pearls." The thing most surprising to us is the number of people who don't seem to get it. Part of the reason is the immense challenge in being able to reach through all the noise of people's everyday lives. Part of it, too, is of having to overcome the ingrained religious culture that prevents people from being open to the concepts of the emerging church. Change in general is hard for most people to accept. Proposed changes to the way in which they worship are even harder. People love their traditions and want to keep them. What they have to understand is that the emerging church is not a threat to tradition; it is a means of strengthening tradition by bringing more people to the faith.

An important pillar of the emerging church is the concept of *nondualistic* thinking. Educating the congregation on this has been Pastor Len's most recent initiative and we daresay, his largest challenge to date. The concept of *dualistic* thinking, of employing a mind-set that categorizes and divides, has been ingrained into our lives from shortly after birth. We're taught at an early age that there are friends and enemies, even if a person designated as an enemy has done nothing to us. We're taught that there are winners and losers and that, heaven forbid, we will never belong in the losing camp. We're taught that some folks are "our kind" and others not, particularly if they're not of the same faith/denomination.

Telling people that this attitude is not only unnecessary but also is flat-out wrong is enough to elicit a collective, "Huh?"

Nondualistic thinking is the means by which we tear down those barriers separating us, as individuals, as families, and as members of the body of Christ. It is a key component for outreach, for inviting in the very people for whom the emerging church was created—the doubters, the questioners, unchurched. By being able to say to them, "All are welcomed" regardless of their socioeconomic heritage, by telling them we don't care what their religious or nonreligious background was before they walked through the door, by admitting up front that we don't have all the answers but that's okay ... because faith is trusting in something you can never know for certain. This is what nondualistic thinking is all about.

We are truly on the cutting edge of not only a new

movement but in the overall Church, one in which we return to our roots and rediscover the mysticism that was for so long a tradition within it.

This literally is a *Back to the Future* movement, one that will rejuvenate the church for generations to come.

• Ann Umbaugh

We are children of the light. This we are told; this we affirm. But those of us who are aware of our flaws can find light harsh and unforgiving. We find more comfort in the glow of a fire, the twinkle of stars, and the lamps of fireflies than a radiant beam.

We come, then, to the *pearls of God* because we find the soft glow inviting. The darkened church, the candlelight, the intimate calm allows us to forgive our own flaws to absorb the words we hear: the words of acceptance and love. We are allowed to have secrets just between ourselves and our Lord. We find a refuge from the busyness of the world where we may receive, reflect, and respond.

Sunday-morning worship can be a glorious experience, but it often lacks time for listening—listening not to music and gospel, but to God's own voice in our hearts.

For those of us raised in the Lutheran tradition, there is great value in taking intentional time away from routine to hear in a new way. For those not accustomed to our rituals but who thirst for God's love, the quiet setting and relaxed pace of *pearls of God* are less intimidating, more accessible.

Is there a sweeter sight during a dark night than a light in the window? If Sunday worship is our sunny picnic, *pearls of God* is our light in the window.

Parallel Realities

I gravitate toward the word parallels. *They lead to multiple destinations along diverse tracks without fatal intersections. New horizons give the impression that the parallels eternally come closer together as each traveler brings new and imaginative creations. All the travelers on all the tracks can get off the trains of thought and mingle at the stations, perhaps in Heuristicville.*

In normal topical conversation we may reply with phrases such as, "This characteristic is universal," meaning that the characteristic is "all there is." The idea of more than one universe, more than one *everything*, is considered by many to be an impossibility. This confined stance is appropriate in some contexts, such as referring to those portions of everything we can access.

But theoretical developments now qualify the

interpretation of *universal,* giving way to other terms that capture expanding possibilities of reality. Parallel universes or parallel worlds or multiple universes or alternate universes are synonymous, all among the words heard to consider not just *our reality* but a spectrum of others that may be touchstones.

Theoretical studies on the quantum properties of black holes suggest that all we experience is a holographic projection of *something* that is taking place on a distant surface that surrounds us.

Greek philosopher Plato likened this kind of view in his "Allegory of the Cave," describing prisoners who have spent their entire lives chained to the wall of a dark cavern, basically a man cave. Behind the prisoners burns a flame, and between the flame and the prisoners parade objects that cast shadows onto a wall in the prisoners' field of view.

These shadows, two-dimensional, are the only things that the prisoners have ever seen, their only reality. Because they are shackled, they are prevented from perceiving the three-dimensional world or realms behind them. This world they cannot see is a dimension rich with complexity and is capable of explaining all that they *do* see.

Plato's allegory leads us to contemporary theoretical studies; for example, perhaps all of us are living in a huge cosmic cave that was created in the first moments of existence.

This is so intriguing to me! It brings edge-thinking to the possibility of a parallel level of reality!

This is so dynamic for me that I seem to return to the cosmically friendly coffeehouse with dim lights. I can even now sense the odor of the drawn, musty drapes. This hazy, nebulous potential parallel reality relates curiously to nebulae, the mists or clouds, or even the dust in interstellar space!

The traditional story goes like this: "The universe came into being during a big bang that started from an infinitely dense point." We can follow this traditional story by standing on top of a mountain in Colorado or by standing in northern Indiana where some people likely believe that the earth is indeed flat and look out and notice that the universe out there appears to exist in three spatial dimensions and one of time, referred to as three-dimensional universe.

But recent calculations, as reported in *Scientific American*, introduce us to the possibility of tracking the start of the universe back to an era *before* the big bang, an era with an *additional* dimension of space.

In this expanded scenario, this three-dimensional

universe is only the shadow of a world with four spatial dimensions, proposing that our entire universe came into being during a stellar implosion in this supra-universe that created a three-dimensional shell around a four-dimensional black hole. Our universe is that shell.

So, perhaps like Plato's prisoners, we have been believing our world is three-dimensional when we actually are a holographic image from the fourth dimension (Afshordi, Mann, and Pourhasan, 2014).

Four-dimensional space deals with a concept called *hyperspace*. Even supernatural phenomenon could possibly be explored with higher dimensional physics. For example, we may be curious and entertain that perhaps God exists in the fourth dimension.

The allegory of the cave theory concerns human perception. Plato claimed that knowledge gained through the senses is no more than opinion and that in order to have real knowledge, we must gain it through philosophical reasoning. This means that Plato distinguishes between people who mistake sensory knowledge for the truth and people who really *do* see the truth.

This theory purports that the cave represents people who believe that knowledge or perception of reality comes from what we see and hear, empirical evidence. But as portrayed in a number of chapters of this book, sense perception may be only a shadow because sense perception may not represent that which is external.

Many theories surround this concept. A favorite one of mine proposes that each time there is more than one possible outcome for an action, the universe splits up so that *all* succeeding events happen, each in a slightly different reality. This means that there are many duplicates of each one of us, but none of them is exactly like us in terms of experiences. I, for example, may turn left, while my duplicate turns right. I will perceive trees, but my duplicate will perceive a lake.

We have possibly had sense perceptions that document this theory because, again, sense perception, be it of a three-dimensional world or of a four-dimensional world, likely does not have direct access to the external world(s). This hinges on the foundational position that sense perception does not directly represent that which is external. It is therefore possible that our perceptions are generated indirectly by *both* three-dimensional and four-dimensional worlds, parallel realities.

I was on a silent retreat at one of my favorite monasteries, the *Abbey of Gethsemani,* Trappist, Kentucky. It was the first week of my three-month/three-dimensional and perhaps four-dimensional sabbatical that would ultimately bring Linda and me to Amsterdam, Helsinki, Estonia, Germany, and Hong Kong.

It's difficult to say in words why it's always so good to be at Gethsemani. The only thing I can say is, "It's because the abbey's church always smells like God. Perhaps it's because I love their brown bread."

The abbey provides a haunting emotion for me—not only because of the nostalgic scents and the eerie silence, but it was here that I turned right into the lounge where I was introduced to the possibility of being a Reinhartz scholar at Lutheran Theological Southern Seminary in Columbia, South Carolina.

Sure enough. That was right! My mentor for my ensuing ecumenical studies there was former Lutheran presiding bishop, James Crumley.

It was also at Gethsemani that a number of us pastors were when Operation Desert Storm started. We left the serenity and isolation of this strict order Trappist rule of silence monastery that night for a pub located by a junction of two railroads with a television.

Almost twenty years later, I arrived at 9:33 p.m. I came up the walk lined with shadows of the tombstones of the cemetery. I had been told to ring the bell if I arrived after eight. The voice on the intercom asked for my name, then assured me that he would be down soon.

Brother Rene opened the door; his hospitality reflected many years of devotion. He looked up my name and said that my room was number 2020. This sounded good, for I desired to have some very clear visionary times here. I would enter through the iron gate leading through a monastic garden, up to the second floor of the south wing. At breakfast the next morning, I avoided Grape Nuts, far too noisy in silence. The oatmeal wasn't the greatest, but it was silent. Hash would have been quiet also while I hashed over my thoughts, but they didn't have any. It was obvious to choose bananas over apples.

A few days later, I asked a retreatant from Campbellsville, Kentucky, to take my picture here at the monastery with my camera. He consented but first asked if my name was Sellers. I said no, not wanting to say too much here at the monastery. He said, "Well, I know a guy from Loretto, and you look just like him. I really thought that you are him. In fact, there is nothing different about you. Even your head is the same."

I thought about asking him if my head and Sellers's head were of different dimensions but decided that would be too far out.

This was intriguing, especially having been told by someone else here that they had heard that I was a Lutheran bishop—and then being told by a person working at the gift shop here that she had seen me here only about a year ago. All of these parallels brought back memories of Fred in New Albany, Indiana.

I was told about him by the short-of-breath manager of the Singer Sewing Shop in New Albany as he came running and jumping toward me, saying, "I saw him! I saw him!"

I said, "Who? Who?"

He said, "Your duplicate! Your duplicate!" He was sew excited!

Fred and I really do look like parallel beings. Occasionally he and I would, or at least we seemed to, have coffee together. I would usually enter the coffee shop through the left door, and Fred would enter through the right door. To this day, I always enter through left doors.

We would sit on opposite sides of what I perceived to be a table. This setting was much like sitting in a coffee shop in front of a mirror, except we would carry on a conversation with each other, each of us responding to the other as we would lift our coffee mugs and drink at *different* times. I held my coffee mug with my right hand, he with his left.

One day his mother thought that I was her son. I told her that I was not. Lucky for Fred, she finally believed me.

Another memory goes back to downtown Louisville. Bill Clinton's political bus tour of the United States had just arrived. As he came out of what was perceived to be a bus, I noticed a gathering of Roman Catholic parishioners protesting about something that liberal Lutherans would not. I saw them intently approaching me. A couple of them said, "Father, it's so good seeing you here … and thanks for presiding at mass last week."

I said, "It's good to perceive you … but I'm a Lutheran pastor, and I never was there!"

They distanced themselves from me a little, perhaps wondering why I would not believe them by pretending to be a Lutheran.

Not more than two years later a Roman Catholic priest from their community attended a funeral at the blended Lutheran/Episcopal parish where I was serving. Sure enough—parallels. I noticed as he left the parking lot he turned left, and I turned right.

Some years later, at the monastery, on a beautiful sunny Sunday day, I decided to drive the twelve miles to Loretto to see if I could find a coffee shop without mirrors. Loretto, home of Maker's Mark whiskey, is a small enough community, so I could perhaps just drive along a street, or perhaps both, in town and see what appeared.

Not perceiving a coffee shop, I stopped at a small grocery store. I asked a checker if I could use a phone book. He pointed to one behind lane two. I immediately picked up this one-sixteenth-inch-thick book. It took little time to reach the S section; I nearly missed it, almost getting into both yellow pages.

I could not believe the number of Sellers listings! I randomly picked one address, asked where this road was, got directions, turned left, and started the investigation.

I drove the 1996 Olds Bravada carefully down the narrow highway and turned left again, and all of a sudden, there it was! I had heard so much about them over the years—the sisters of Loretto! Right in front of me was the Loretto Motherhouse of Nerinx, Kentucky!

I decided to change my direction for a bit. I turned left again and drove up the drive, turning right into the sisters' property, parked, and entered the impressive complex, which houses about one hundred nuns. I talked with several people and then had a surprise of my life!

As I turned right into a room with literature, there was a cabinet with about five old-style audio cassettes on its top. A sign read, "Everything free on cabinet top."

Several weeks earlier I had read that a Franciscan priest, Father Richard Rohr of Albuquerque, New Mexico, had presided at the Thomas Mass in Helsinki during its twentieth anniversary year. He's of the OFM, Order of Friars Minor. I know many OFMs, but not him. But the Franciscan connect was really neat! A Franciscan! Celebrating a Lutheran mass, in Helsinki, with Pastor Olli Valtonen, where Linda and I would be in a few weeks participating in the Thomas Mass with Olli Valtonen!

I looked at these old-style audio cassettes. One label said, "Come to the Table: Faith in our Post-Modern Culture—Richard Rohr." I could scarcely believe what I was seeing! How did this happen? In what dimension was this place? Why did I turn left a number of times and then right? What was I doing there? Why was I there?

Having been at the monastery for several days in silence except for the crunching sound of Grape Nuts without enough milk, I actually internalized all of these huge questions, not saying a thing. In complete silence, then, I hastily but carefully opened the old cassette case to read perhaps why Fr. Rohr celebrated the Thomas Mass.

The 1996 entry (surprisingly the year my old Olds Bravada was manufactured perhaps in the three-dimensional world) said this:

Father Rohr describes what we are up against in our postmodern culture. He describes our culture with its absence of meaning patterns and suggests that unless we have one Lord, we will simply adopt our American culture of skepticism as our belief system.

I enjoyed the surprises in this place—and the connections! This was like listening to Olli Valtonen and Richard Rohr, saying stuff across the table from each other.

I left the room and had a pleasant half-hour conversation with Sister Mary, the nun who found the light switches for the church so I could take a picture with my camera after three ladies couldn't find them and had phoned a fourth, who didn't answer. I drove back to the highway, where there were two guys talking with each other out of their pickups' side windows near a drop-off.

They looked like each other. As I talked with them, they amazingly mentioned "out of the blue" that many people thought they looked like each other. They said they were related … somehow.

With this astonishing segue and a little hesitation, I asked them if they knew any Sellers. They said, "Many." I said that I was not narcissistic but that I was told that I looked like a Sellers and made a left turn to this area where some Sellers live. So, a little slowly, I said, "Do I look like a Sellers?"

They said, "Absolutely."

I said, "Which one?"

They said, "All of them."

They said that one of the Sellers runs a used furniture store in Loretto.

I stopped by the locked store and looked in the windows. One of the windows was ajar. Darkness was approaching. Several rooms were hauntingly lighted dimly. A slight breeze brought a musty odor from the old, drawn drapes. As I left, I looked back and perceived my reflection in the window of the left door. Silence filled the store, at least for a while.

Curious.

Bibliography

Afshordi, Mann, and Pourhasan. "The Black Hole That Birthed the Big Bang." *Scientific American,* July 15, 2014.

Cox. *Religion in the secular city: toward a postmodern theology.* Holiday House, 1985.

Einstein. *"Death of a Genius."* LIFE Magazine, May 2, 1955, 64.

Entwistle. *The fashioned body: fashion, dress, and modern social theory.* Malden, MA: Polity Press, 2000.

Fox. *The coming of the cosmic Christ: the healing of Mother Earth and the birth of a global renaissance.* New York: HarperCollins, 1988.

Fox. *Christian mystics: 365 readings and meditations.* New World Library, 2011.

Fuller. *Spiritual, but not religious: understanding unchurched America.* Oxford: Oxford Univ. Press, 2001.

Gedicks, and Hendrix. "Religious Experience in the Age of Digital Reproduction." *St. John's Law Review,* Winter (2005).

Gendlin. "Introduction to Thinking at the Edge" (2004) (in The Folio, Vol 19 No 1, 2004).

Kashdan and Silvia, *"Curiosity and Interest the Benefits of Thriving on Novelty and Challenge,"* Positive Psychology (2nd Ed.), 2009.

Kashdan. *Curious?: discover the missing ingredient to a fulfilling life.* Harper Collins, 2009.

Keillor. *Pontoon: A Lake Wobegon Novel.* New York: Penguin Group (USA) Inc., Viking Press, 2007, p. 185.

Knitter, *The Myth of Christian Uniqueness—Toward a Pluralistic Theology of Religions,* Maryknoll, 1988.

Lanzetta. *The other side of nothingness: toward a theology of radical openness.* Albany, NY: State University of New York Press, 2001.

McCrae. *"Personality trait development from age 12 to age 18: Longitudinal, cross-sectional and cross-cultural analyses." Journal of Personality and Social Psychology,* 2002, 1456–1468.

Nicholas, and Salter. *The vision of God.* New York: Cosimo, 2007.

Panikkar. *The Unknown Christ Of Hinduism: Towards an Ecumenical Christophany* (1981 Maryknoll, NY. Orbis Books.)

Rasmussen. *Earth community earth ethics.* Maryknoll, NY: Orbis Books, 1996.

Rohr, "Creation as the Body of God," *Radical Grace*, Vol. 23, No. 2 (Center for Action and Contemplation: April–June 2010), 3, 22.

Trueheart. "The Next Church." *The Atlantic,* August, 1996.

About the Author

Len Jepson sets the stage for peaceful, better lives with his improvisational personality. He develops and maintains relationships that are built on compassionate models that are supportive instead of competitive. In other words, improvisation is open to enjoy the treasures of diverse people and communities. Instead of looking out for one's own isolated beliefs or views, improvisation is a collaborative effort that delivers new life experiences for everyone.

On an average day, social environments and relationships change hundreds of times, especially in recent times with our ever-increasing pluralistic cultures. Improvisational leadership responds to less-than-ideal considerations for peace and justice by introducing relaxed and open thinking, choosing to be optimistic by seeking creative possibilities.

He is motivated with the improvisational model, the art of embracing the surprising instead of the expected results. This teaches how to take risks instead of being satisfied with the ways things are. Improvisation develops a contagious mind-set promoting curiosity with radical openness, flexibility, and the desire to build strong relationships, the building of bridges instead of barriers. His administrative disciplines for communities bring richer, clearer, and wider parameters.

With his growing passion for ecumenical and then interreligious leadership, he was a Lutheran synodical representative in major local and national dialogues. He also served a blended Lutheran/Episcopal parish and taught world religions at Bellarmine University.

Living on the border of Michigan and Indiana, called Michiana, Len's personality spills over and mixes with new friendships. People not only are brought to laughter with sermons filled with puns, but they become punsters as well; his office became known as the training room for kids, with a model railroad circling his desk.

Len's improvisational resources were enhanced in 2008 as he studied emerging Christianity, which considers the dynamics of changing cultures. These travels included studies in Helsinki, Germany, and Hong Kong.

Len and his wife, Linda, live in Mishawaka, Indiana. Their daughter and son-in-law, Abby and Mat Berry, live in Englewood, Colorado.

TRUE DIRECTIONS

An affiliate of Tarcher Perigee

OUR MISSION

Tarcher Perigee's mission has always been to publish books that contain great ideas. Why? Because:

GREAT LIVES BEGIN WITH GREAT IDEAS

At Tarcher Perigee, we recognize that many talented authors, speakers, educators, and thought-leaders share this mission and deserve to be published – many more than Tarcher Perigee can reasonably publish ourselves. True Directions is ideal for authors and books that increase awareness, raise consciousness, and inspire others to live their ideals and passions.

Like Tarcher Perigee, True Directions books are designed to do three things: inspire, inform, and motivate.

Thus, True Directions is an ideal way for these important voices to bring their messages of hope, healing, and help to the world.

Every book published by True Directions– whether it is non-fiction, memoir, novel, poetry or children's book – continues Tarcher Perigee's mission to publish works that bring positive change in the world. We invite you to join our mission.

For more information, see the True Directions website:

www.iUniverse.com/TrueDirections/SignUp

Be a part of Tarcher Perigee's community to bring positive change in this world! See exclusive author videos, discover new and exciting books, learn about upcoming events, connect with author blogs and websites, and more! www.tarcherbooks.com

TRUE DIRECTIONS
AN AFFILIATE OF TARCHER PERIGEE